Gandhian Ideology
and
Modern World

Gandhian Ideology and Modern World

Edited by

Dr. A.B.S.V. Ranga Rao

GANDHIAN STUDIES CENTRE
Andhra University
Visakhapatnam

AKANSHA PUBLISHING HOUSE
NEW DELHI • GUWAHATI • VISAKHAPATNAM

AKANSHA PUBLISHING HOUSE
4649-B/21, Ansari Road
Daryaganj, New Delhi-110002
Phones: 23268193, 09435116718
Email: ektabooks@yahoo.com
visit us: www.akanshapublishinghouse.com

Gandhian Ideology and Modern World

First Published 2011

ISBN 978-81-8370-295-9

PRINTED IN INDIA

Published by Akansha Publishing House, New Delhi-110002 and printed at Harmain Offset Printers, Delhi.

Contents

Foreword *vii*

Preface *ix*

Acknowledgements *xvii*

Our Contributors *xix*

SECTION I

Ideologies of Gandhi and Other Social Thinkers

1. Lohia's Extension of Gandhian Thought 3
Surendra Mohan

2. The Global Crisis: Gandhi and Lohia 11
Bhagawat Prasad Rath

3. Bose, Gandhi and Ambedkar: Their Ideologies 20
K.Raghu Rama Reddy & A. Hariprasad

4. Confronting Gandhi: Ambedkar Views on Future Religion of Hindus 26
Ch. Y. Sudhakar

5. Gandhi's Views on Non-Violence 36
S.V.G. Choodamani

SECTION - II

Gandhian Ideology: Relevance to Contemporary Society

6. Gandhian Ideology: Relevance to the Contemporary Society 45
M. Lakshmipathi Raju

7. Gandhiji's Contribution to Indian Society: Social Work Perspective 57
Saraswarthi Raju Iyer

8. Gandhi and Social Action: The Educational perspective 68
V.Krishna Murthy & R.V.L.N. Ratnakar

9. The Role of Values in Education in the Context of Globalization: The Gandhian Perspective 84
D. Rama Rao and G. Rajeswari

10. Youth and Global Peace in Gandhian Perspective 93
P. Kishore Kumar & B.Chennaiah

11. Globalization : A Gandhian Perspective 102
K. Visweswara Rao & K. Ananda Kumar

12. Relevance of Gandhian Principles for Sustainable management of Natural Resources 113
P. Usha & S. Pulla Rao

13. The Impact of Gandhism on Indian English literature with special reference to select novels 120
G. Chenna Reddy

14. Gandhi and His Weapon to Rebuild Society 129
P. Kishore Kumar, K. Ravi Kumar, Ch. Ramakrishna & K. Sridevi

Index 135

Foreword

It gives me immense pleasure to write foreword to the volume entitled, 'Gandhian Ideology and Modern World', edited by Dr. A.B.S.V. Ranga Rao, Programme Coordinator, Gandhian Studies Centre. I am glad that the Gandhian studies centre is bringing out in book form, the seminar proceedings and the collection of papers authored by experienced faculty members and scholars of various universities at a time when there is decadence of ethical and human values. The authors attempted to discuss the relevance of Gandhian ideology to remedy the present day evils and manifold crises that have confronted the contemporary world.

Gandhi challenges the deep inequalities he finds in India and offers a powerful defense of autonomy and, alongside a comprehensive critique of western modernity and modernization. He attacks colonialism as well as Untouchablity because each subordinates the individual. Gandhi challenges modernity and modernization because, he sees each disabling men and women, and he confronts violence because, it treats people as a means to be used for the benefit of the powerful.

Gandhiji initiated constructive social welfare programmes designed to remove the evils that had crept into society. His constructive programmes found ready acceptance among people. His concept of constructive work is not merely for producing things; it is the means of educating and spiritualizing man. It means developing self- discipline and self control. Gandhi gave to the world new and revolutionary concepts such as satyagraha (Truth force), sarvodya (Welfare of all) and santhi sena (Peace – Brigade). These Gandhian concepts are found to gain greater relevance in the coming years.

There is, in fact, an endless array of problems that have engulfed the whole world, many of them man- made and need to be tackled in the interest of peace, progress and sustainable development of the entire world. The UNESCO has proclaimed the present decade from 2001-2010 as the decade for peace and

Non- violence. We should eschew the culture of violence and move towards culture of peace.

The paper writers dealt with wide range of issues relating to Gandhian ideology from historical perspective to social justice, democracy, ethical values, non-violence, truth, soul force, global peace, social transformation and social reconstruction.

I find a combination of the papers belonging to various disciplines compiled in this book, reflecting the Gandhian philosophy, with interdisciplinary focus for depicting the various dimensions of Gandhain thought. The issues discussed in this volume are of great concern for social scientists, policy-makers, human rights activists and particularly for these who are working for social transformation, social reconstruction and global peace.

Prof. Beela. Satyanarayana
Vice-Chancellor
Andhra University
Visakhapatnam

Preface

Gandhi envisioned that we have to move towards a no-poverty and no-misery society which will really feed, clothe and provide shelter to everybody and treat everybody in the world as equal and pave the way to live in peace. We should move towards a society where everyone will live in harmony with his neighbor, where everyone will be treated with equal respect, will feel secure, self respect and self-confidence and feels he/she is wanted. Everyone realizes that it is only global peace that will make the human race feel safe and happy. The world today has accepted Gandhi as a model to solve the problems of the present century. In the twenty-first century, the Gandhian concepts are found to gain greater relevance. In fact Gandhian thought is more relevant today than ever before.

The book contains the articles by senior academicians, who have been working in their respective fields and disciplines of Sociology, Social Work, Political Science, Public Administration, Law, History, Philosophy, Literature, Family studies and also in the related areas of Gandhian Thought and Ideology.

This work is divided in two sections.

The first section deals with Ideologies of Gandhi and other Indian social thinkers.

Surendra Mohan holds that Gandhi and Lohia are precisely those thinkers whose ideas, backed by strong political wills, will save human civilization from sure collapse. Fromme describes the marketing-oriented character of the modern man thus "In our time the marketing orientation has been growing rapidly together with the development of a new market that is a phenomenon of the last decades, the personality market. Because of the existence of the personality market, many are coerced to wear a pleasant mask along with the manipulated personality. The military and marketing-oriented characters become doubly dangerous when they are reinforced by each other. Gandhi and Lohia were both votaries of non-violent revolutions. Gandhi's discovery of satyagraha was the greatest gift to the present war and slaughter-prone humanity. By making truth and non-violence as inseparable pair, Gandhi made the military irrelevant for a happiness-seeking world society.

Bhagawat Prasad Rath discusses the global crisis affecting human race; with the deterioration and destruction of nature, rising temperature, climate goes hostile to survival. Toxicity threatens the health of millions. Martin Rees, Royal Society president prophetically declares ..." The decisions that we make, individually or collectively, will determine whether the outcomes of 21st century science are benign or devastating.

Prof. K. Raghu Rama Reddy and Dr. A. Harisprasad make an attempt to compare and contrast the ideologies of Subhas Chandra Bose, Baba Saheb Ambedkar and Mohandas Karamchand Gandhi, the important leaders of Indian National Movement. Netaji Subhas Chandra Bose believed in a strong courageous, brave India and the might of the sword. Gandhi belived in truth and non-violence and the might of the soul. But both worked for the liberation of the motherland. Gandhi preferred cottage industries. Netaji preferred one party rule. Gandhi preferred partyles rule. Gandhi was against fascism and communism. Gandhi and Ambedkar both rejected formal democracy as being inadequate as well as harmful, Gandhi favoured decentralization of democratic set up but Ambedkar showeed his preference for what he called social democracy. However both came down to accept formal democracy as practical proposition. Gandhji was ready to grant all the necessary civic rights to the untouchables but Ambedkar insisted upon autonomous political status of untouchables , and therefore, demanded separate electorate.

Dr. Ch. Y. Sudhakar holds that Ambedkar's life became a continuous fight against Hindu religion to rethink of the ageold practices with disbelief. Gandhi opposed for the creation of any constitutional measures in the name of the special communal constituencies for the dalits as they became the part of the Hindu religion not separate minority groups like that of Muslims and Sikhs. Ambedkar challenged the Hindu authorities allowing the evil practice of untouchability and he dared to author the Indian Constitution liberating many forms of hereditary ill treatment. With bitter experience of untouchability, Ambedkar could not yield to the demands of Gandhi. Dr. Sudhakar observed that Gandhi accepted for the representation of dalits or the depressed classes in the government with adequate general and common constituencies. This shows the way how the depressed classes of India were liberated and saved from the clutches of senseless orthodoxy. This marked the end of the social hegemony of certain sections within Indian society in the name of Hindu religious code of conduct given by Manu.

S.V.G Chodamani discusses in her paper Gandhi's views on Non-violence. The kernel of Gandhi's life message which is eternal and universal and which made him a mahatma is peace and non-violence. The philosophy of Gandhi is mainly based on twin principles, viz.,truth and non-violence. According to Gandhi, non-violence is truthfulness. Truth is inseparable ingredient of non-violence and they are like the two sides of a coin. A person who follows the principles of truth and non-violence knows no defeat in life. Today, we can also unite under a single belief of non- violence and love in order to eradicate the evils that are holding humankind. During his search for truth, he made the discovery of non-violence. Truth and non-violence, gradually, became convertible concepts. The values of truth and non-violence were implanted in him, as a result of his upbringing.

The *Second section* brings out the relevance of Gandhian views and ideology to the contemporary society. Prof. M. Lakshmipathi Raju discusses the Gandhian ideology from social work perspective and finds its relevance to the contemporary professional social work practice. Mahatma Gandhi made significant contribution to social development by his constructive work and programmes, aiming at removal of disabilities of the people at the social, political, economic and spiritual levels. An in-depth study of Gandhian movements will provide a perennial source of inspiration. It should be made an integral part of a programme of social work education. Gandhiji says: "the human body is meant for service, never for indulgence, renunciation is life, indulgence spells death. Service to humanity has been the ideal of all saints and prophets of peace and so for Gandhiji.

When there is breakdown of moral order in society, the professional social workers cannot remain just a 'conscienceless scientism'. It is the duty of the professional social workers as the upholders of universal norms to step in as shown by Gandhi. Gandhi's strategy was that "social transformation should begin with millions of 'non-persons' and 'half persons', marginalized Indian Humanity", living in the outskirts of organized society and below the margins of subsistence within the society". Gandhiji's constructive programme is a comprehensive instrument of reconstruction which specially included the needs of 'non-persons', the outcastes, the half persons, the castaways and the lowliest and the poorest section of human population.

Gandhiji felt that it is necessary to transform society through the individual and by social values of love, non-violence and justice. Social workers must create the conditions which would help the people to be self-reliant and realize the ideals of the purity, honesty and righteousness, fair play, justice and universal tolerance without the loss of individual freedom. Professional social work has to be a way of life, not just a mere profession to earn money, name and fame.

Dr. Saraswathi Raju Iyer highlights Gandhiji's contribution to Indian society from social work perspective. Gandhiji said that he had made the religion of service his own as he felt that god could be realized only through service. He was greatly influenced by Ruskin's book *Unto the Last* which he translated to Gujarati under the title 'Sarvodaya'(Welfare of all). Dr. Saraswathi distinguishes Sarvodaya from the concept of professional social work. The concept of sarvodaya is much order in origin. The concept of professional social work is about a century old. Sarvodaya is a broader concent than social work. Its goal is welfare of all and creation of stateless and classless society, through Bhoodan, Gramodan, Gramswaraj, Santhi Sena and non-violence. Social work aims at helping individuals within their own selves or in their own environment to solve their problems. Sarvodaya emphasizes truth and non-violence and the basic goodness of the man; social work while upholding the values of dignity of man, emphasizes also acceptance of individual's right to self-determination and confidentiality. The values of social work are not based in particular individual's philosophies of life and action;

they have developed on the basis of experience of practitioners over a period of time.

Prof. V. Krishna Murthy and RVLN Ratnakar Rao, hold that the basic education or Nai Talim(New Education) stands as the unique contribution of Gandhi. Gandhi advocated a new system of education appropriate to the Indian socio-economic conditions. The Basic education involves socio-economic activities like involvement of students in learning a craft and developing Kitchen garden to improve self sufficiency of the school. Gandhi defined education as the "all round drawing out of the best in child and man-body, mind and spirit." (*The Harijan*, 31-3-37, p.197). This broader view of education made basic education holistic in the sense that it is not merely literacy but capacity –building and personality development as well as intellectual development and character development as the criterion in the progress of the society as a whole. He says what better book can there be than the book of humanity. He made humanity as the focus in his scheme of educational plan. No one realized better than Gandhi the tragedy of speculative thought without social action and of social action without true reflection. What should, attract a social scientist to Gandhi is his insistence on primacy of rational thought as the basis of social action . Gandhi's whole theory of basic education was derived from the belief in the value of work. He was not prepared to concede that culture only came from books.

Dr. Rama Rao Dhramana and Dr.Rajeswari Gulipilli discuss in their paper the present values in education in the context of globalization from the Gandhian perspective. The authors observe that the concept of Gandhian education is relevant to meet the needs and demands of the 21st century society experiencing the globalization process. Gandhiji advocated that education should develop the child's individuality fully and harmoniously so that he is able to realize the ultimate aim of life which is truth or god. Gandhiji has himself explained education- as "by education I mean an all-round drawing out of the best in children and man's body, mind and sprit." Gandhiji's scheme of education is known as basic education. His philosophy of education is a harmonious blending of idealism, naturalism and pragmatism. The Iswarbhai Patel committee feels that the principle of basic education as evolved by Mahatma Gandhi and accepted in the Kothari Commission report with the stress on work education, need to find a central place in the education system. Mahatma Gandhi while emphasizing education as a means of developing the potentialities of the child and his/her character also emphasized that the social relevance of modern science and technology should be seriously considered in the context of poverty and degradation of millions of Indian people.

Dr. P. Kishore Kumar and B. Chennaiah in their paper stated that the entire humanity is craving for peace at different levels such as individual, social, communal, national and international levels. Gandhiji warned youngsters against misinterpreting religions. All religions such as Hinduism, Christianity, Islam, Buddhism, Jainism etc., have preached peace and harmony. Mahatma Gandhi himself made skillful use of Satyagraha to achieve peace and harmony. He always believed that peace contains a negative and a positive sense. The absence of configuration, elimination of wars, absence of conflicts between different classes, castes, religions and nations are in a negative sense and love, rest, mental equilibrium, harmony, cooperation, unity, happiness are the positive indices of peace. There is a war being waged, a war where the youth of nation will actively participate, a war of knowledge of science vs peace of mind, a war of education vs character building, a war of professional management vs social commitment. The able-bodied soldiers namely the youth of India are being lead by none else but by beloved Mahatma as the Commander-in-Chief.

Prof. K. Visweswara Rao and K. Anada Rao observ in their paper that Gandhi has seldom written about strictly modern process of globalization, because present day modernization was far away in his time. But he has reflected on related areas of international federation, world peace, and exploitation of the weak by the stronger nation. As such, Gandhi has a vision for unity of mankind, universal brotherhood and "living association of human beings" the world over. The modern surging ahead in multi- media technology bringing in its wake a global transformation. Entire world has now become a "global village" writings and sayings of Mahatma Gandhi and majority of commentators and critics of Gandhian philosophy have shown not only inherent but also explicit significance of the idea of oneness of humanity, individual's dignity and self-reliance for swaraj in Gandhi's practical idealist perspective of politics. His experiments, however have led him to evolve, according to several commentators and analysts like S.C. Gangal, Mahendra Kumar, Raghaven Iyer, Savita Singh, Ramjee Singh, Johan Yaltung and others predominantly non- violent state as his second best ideal and a non-violent society as his ultimate ideal for establishing a vibrantly creative global and just political ethos where cooperation, equality and non-violence has replaced exploitation, inequality and bloody warfare and mutual hatred.

Dr. P. Usha and Dr. S. Pulla Rao discuss in their paper the relevance of Gandhian principles for sustainable management of natural resources. In the context of the present scenario of global environment problems, one should rely on Gandhian philosophy in managing the natural resources and thereby protecting our environment from the degradation. Gandhiji had forecasted the threat to resources a century ago and advocated the need for sustainable management of resources and suggested how could be the resources managed in a sustainable manner for the future benefit. Gandhiji opined that human greediness and reckless consumption of resources cause depletion of natural resources. Gandhiji's views on the exploitation of nature is clearly stated enough in his famous saying that the earth has enough to satisfy everyone's needs but not every one's greed.

Dr. G. Chenna Reddy critically examined the impact of Gandhism on Indian English literature with special reference to select novels. R.K.Narayn's "Waiting for the Mahatma" is an important novel, which deals with the freedom movement as background. The novel deals with some of the important incidents during the Quit India Movement, where Gandhi is character. Chaman Nahal's "Quartet", which is a "Gandhian Saga", deals with most of the major incidents and moments of the freedom struggle including the non cooperation moment during 1920 and 1922. The novel, "The crown and the loin cloth" begins with the return journey of Gandhi from South Africa to India in the ship S.S. Aribia after the completion of his successful sojourn. He has successfully tested his newly found principle satyagraha with which he fought against the British in South Africa. Chaman Nahal introduces historical characters and events in the first chapter of the novel. Gandhi recollects the past incidents of his life as to how he spent two decades in South Africa and how he neglected to show love and affection towards his family members, while he was sailing from South Africa to India. The author confines to narration of the historical characters and incidents at the opening chapter of the novel. Nahal develops the story imposing Gandhism through the character of the Sunil and extremism through the character of the Rakesh simultaneously. Using historical events and actions, Nahal is inclined to accept the victory of Gandhism over extremism. The village Ajitha is stirred with the call of non-cooperation moment by Gandhi.

Dr. P. Kishore Kumar, K. Ravikumar, Ch. Ramakrishna and K. Sridevi describe in their paper about Gandhi's weapons to rebuild society. They have explained in the paper, the Gandhian way of upliftment of downtrodden. The destitute, the girijans, cr untouchable are Gandhi's daridranarayans, the beggar and any other socially handicapped groups of people constitute the class of downtrodden. Appearance of Gandhi on Indian scene in early part of this century virtually brought new hopes and aspirations as well as bright future for the weaker sections, namely harijans, girijans, sudras, lepers , women and all those who belong to weaker sections. Gandhi took up the cause of untouchables, sudras, women, tribals, lepers and the poor irrespective of their caste and occupation.

Editor

Acknowledgements

At the outset, I deem it a privilege to express our deep sense of gratitude to Prof. Beela Satyanarayana, former Vice-Chancellor, Andhra University for inspiring and guiding us in running the Centre for the last three years.

We thank him for his help and appreciation of the efforts of the Gandhian Studies Centre.

We are indebted to Prof. S.V. Sudhakar, Vice-Chancellor, Dr. B.R. Ambedkar University, Etcherla, and In-Charge Vice-Chancellor of Andhra University for writing who is instrumental in making the Centre a reality.

It is also our bounden duty to acknowledge our respectful thanks to Prof. G. Hara Gopal, Central University, Hyderabad who has been a source of inspiration and for his encouragement and guidance and offering his valuable insights in the development of Gandhi literature from our Centre.

I owe a great debt of thanks to Sri K.S. Sastry, Secretary, Gandhi Centre, Visakhapatnam for his kind help and encouragement.

I express my thanks to Prof. K. Sreeranjani Subba Rao, Head of the department of Politics & Public Administration, Prof. G. Veerraju, Head of the Department of Philosophy and Prof. K. Visweswara Rao, Dean of Examinations, Andhra University for their constant support and valuable suggestions as members of the Advisory Committee of the Gandhian Studies Centre in running the Centre.

I immensely thank our dynamic former Vice-Chancellors of Andhra University, Prof. Y.C. Simhadri and Prof. L. Venugopal Reddy for their encouragement and also to the Registrar, P.V.G.D. Prasada Reddy for providing timely suggestions.

I must express my gratitude and appreciation to all the learned contributors who contributed their analytical articles to this volume.

I heartfully acknowledge the help of University Grants Commission, New Delhi for their generous financial help to the centre.

My thanks are due to Dr. P. Kishore Kumar, Research Associate, Gandhian Studies Centre, for his support for facilitating the preparation and editing of the book.

I thank .our publishers, Akansha Publishing House, New Delhi for their promptness in bringing of out this book in so short a time.

I thank all others who in some way or the other, directly or indirectly contributed for the publication of the present volume.

Prof. A.B.S.V. Ranga Rao

Our Contributors

Surendra Mohan, Former MP, Veteran Socialist, Andhra Pradesh

Bhagwat Prasad Rath, Freedom Fighter & Gandhian, Rayagada, Orissa.

Prof. K. Raghurama Reddy, Department of Political Univeristy, Kakatiya Univeristy, Warangal.

Dr. A. Hariprasad, Assocaite Professor, Department of Political Univeristy, Kakatiya Univeristy, Warangal.

Ch. Y Sudhakar, Research Associate, Gandhian Studies Centre, GITAM,Visakhapatnam.

Dr. S.V.G. Choodamani, Research Scholar, Department of Philosophy, Sri Venkateswara University, Tirupathi, Chittoor Dist, AP

Professor M.Lakshmipathi Raju, Department of Social Work, M.R. PG College, Viziangaram

Mr. Saraswati Raju Iyer, Assistant Professor, Dept. of Sociology and Social Work, Nagarjuna University, Guntur.

Sona Kanti Barua, Renowned Gandhian,Orissa.

Professor V.Krishna Murthy, Dept. of Education (Rtd.), Andhra University, Visakkapatnam.

Dr.R.V.L.N. Ratnakara Rao, Department of Physical Education, Andhra University, Visakhapatnam

Dr. Rama Rao Dharmana, Assistant Professor, Department of Sociology, Andhra University, Visakhapatnam.

Dr. Rajeswari Gulipilli, Head and Senior Lecturer, Department of English, MR College of Education, Vizianagaram.

Dr. P. Kishore Kumar, Research Associate, Gandhian Studies Centre, Andhra University.

Badugu Chenniah, Assistant Programme Co-ordinator, CHILDLINE, AP, Chennai

Professor K. Visweswara Rao, Department of Social Work, Andhra University, Visakhapatnam

Dr. K. Ananda Kumar, Research Scholar, Department of Education, Andhra University, Visakhapatnam.

Dr. P. Usha, Assistant Professor, Dr.Durga Bai Deshmukh Centre for Women's Studies, Andhra University, Visakhapatnam.

Dr. S. Pulla Rao, Reader & Hea, Deptt. of Economics, Mrs.AVN College, Visakhapatnam.

Dr. G. Chenna Reddy, Assistant Professor, Department of English, Nagarjuna University, Guntur.

Mr. Koti Ravi Kumar, Research Scholar, Department of Social Work, Andhra University,

Mr.Ch. Ramakrishna, Research Scholar, Department of Social Work, Andhra University,

Mrs. K. Sridevi, Research Scholar, Department of Social Work, Andhra University.

SECTION - 1

IDEOLOGIES OF GANDHI AND OTHER SOCIAL THINKERS

1

Lohia's Extension of Gandhian Thought

Surendra Mohan

Dr. Ram Manohar Lohia described himself as a heretical Gandhian. This was in the context of his rejection of governmental Gandhism which he strongly denounced and opposed, and the monastic Gandhism which disappointed him for having become an adjunct of governmental Gandhism. Having seen the descent of India into a country of massive poverty where inequalities are the highest in the world while its ruling elite lives off the people in the most ostentatious style comparable to the richest of the world, one would easily find the seeds of his anger. Governmental Gandhism, he complained, continued the old order, while the Gandhian precept was to assault it. As for monastic Gandhism, its failure to resist the Gandhians in authority and its resort to prayers, seminars, conferences and peace marches disheartened him. It may however be pointed out that after his premature demise, some of the monastic Gandhians fought a hard, non-violent battle for total revolution and against the imposition of internal emergency in the country under the leadership of his old comrade Jai Prakash Narayan, and to that extent, upheld his faith in civil disobedience. However, the blatant injustice and inequality in the society, the trigger- happy responses of those in authority even against those resisting it peacefully and the mode of development which has displaced millions from their homes should have made every follower of Gandhi to use the weapon of civil resistance which, as Lohia said, was Gandhi's greatest gift to mankind.

Civil disobedience on a mass scale was organised by Gandhi during the freedom struggle. This non-violent weapon was employed in Champaran, Kheda and Bardoli as well. Lohia was keen that all kinds of injustice should be resisted non-violently. The satyagrahas led by him in Kodur in Karnataka, Fatehgarh in U.P. and Imphal in Manipur were among the more well known. During those early years after freedom, socialists offered non violent resistance in a large number of pockets, mainly on issues related to the peasant. The Pardi satyagraha led by Asoka Mehta in Gujarat was also a massive agitation. Lohia also thought of permanent civil resistance. Civil resistance by individuals, as his satyagraha in Alabama in the USA, was no less necessary. As for foreign invasion, he said that if ten per cent of the people are ready to sacrifice themselves in non- violent resistance, the invasion could be repulsed. He moulded the Socialist Party which he led from 1955 till his demise into a brigade of civil resisters but was not satisfied with the results, as his ideal was that they not only launch it internally, but a stage should come when a large number of people the world over should offer satyagraha for the creation of a world parliament. However, he never favoured any talk of a world government or transcendence of national sovereignties unless equal productivity was achieved internationally and every person succeeded in getting a decent standard of living.

Gandhi had said that his life was his message. Lohia was therefore keen that the messge should be incorporated in the socialist movement. Continuous action, simple living, a keen desire to experiment as also learn from others' experiences, fight against injustice, coupled with constructive work and compassion were the qualities of Gandhi's living. Gandhi was in favour of a technology that human beings could comprehend, manage and control, a habitat which was self-sufficient and under control of the inhabitants, and direct democracy. Another precept of Gandhi, dear to Lohia, was the purity of the means and their close correspondence with the ends. All these ideas became part of the socialist movements. As for example, he introduced a resolution in the National Conference of the Socialist Party held at Patna in 1949, called for reconstruction of the society though constructive work and symbolized it by spade, just as the jail stood as a symbol of civil disobedience and vote as one for elections. For quite some time, hundreds of party workers devoted themselves to constructive work. The Sewa Pathak of the Rashtra Sewa Dal, the Yusuf Meherally Centre and a few Bharat Yatra Kendras established by Chandra Shekhar are prime examples of constructive work in which socialist workers are still engaged.

Lohia practiced kanchan mukti in his personal life, and taught the value of simplicity to his followers. In fact, most of the leaders and workers of the socialist movement generally lived, and continue to live, simple lives. The technology which Lohia advocated was the power driven small machine, and he found justification for it by showing that monstrous machines were wasteful, much too complicated and incomprehensible for their users, were uncontrollable by them, were centralized so that they stood for inequality and were not feasible in capital scarce countries of the southern hemisphere inhabited by the coloured people. He pointed out that the western technology had built nuclear weapons which, as of now, count more than 25 000 in the possession mainly of the USA and Russia. This technology is hugely capital expensive, and had to be based on the exploitation of other people. The German revolutionary Rosa Luxemburg had argued a hundred years ago in 1912 that unless a country captured the resources and the markets of another county, indstrialisation was not possible. She thereby refuted Lenin's theory that imperialism was the last stage of capitalism. Dr. Lohia also wrote on similar lines in his famous essay 'Economics after Marx'. Americo-Europeans, all white, have been producing very large quantities of goods because the Afro-Asians and South Americans buy them. In order that this state of affairs continues and, additionally, they capture, for all time to come, the natural resources of the countries of the South, the process of globalization and its institutional form, the WTO, had been set up by the Euro Americans. The Marxists who ruled Russia for over seven decades employed the same technology, thereby sharing the prosperity of Western Europe and the USA. On the other hand, their rule in China has brought immense misery to hundreds of millions of people as in India. Lohia therefore said that Marxism had impacted on Europe and Asia in two different ways. But, he also found that Marxism was as irrelevant for the southern hemisphere as was capitalism.

But, Lohia, unlike Gandhi, saw the Welfare State coming

up in the West which had banished hunger, destitution and want from it. That this had been achieved by democratic socialism impressed him, and he was not as dismissive of western civilization as Gandhi was. He contrasted the social security available in those courtiers with the hunger, squalor and filth in the counties of the south from Cairo to Canton, and blamed the quiescent culture among the coloured people for not staging revolutions against these conditions. Nevertheless, during the last decade, South America has changed greatly as people's revolts have brought down the regimes which were following the policies of the World Bank and were proxies for the rulers in Washington. In most cases, the overthrow of these governments has been occasioned by peaceful popular protests, and the situation is still fluid.

The non violent resistance against the WTO by thousands of people wherever its conferences have taken place are in protest of the vast disparities among nations which have increased manifold during the last fifteen years after the founding of the WTO. The ever improving technologies of the west have created a much bigger disparity between the productive capacity of a western worker and his Indian counterpart. Lohia had foreseen it and therefore insisted that while full employment was necessary, no less necessary was equality of production between the two, along with a corresponding mode of production and ownership. This equality was impossible of achievement on the basis of transference of western technology to the South because, apart from its wastefulness, it would require unthinkably huge resources, and the eco system would be even more severely jeopardized. Hence, the only logical way was the adoption of small unit machine which was eco friendly, labour intensive and capital scarce.

A state of affairs in which such sharp disparities grow ever sharper is not conducive to peace They are not only economic, they are militaristic also. Moreover, the structure of the Security Council, which as Dr. Lohia said was dominated by five Brahmins, among whom only one was coloured, multiplied the disparities. These disparities have resulted in the wars against Iraq and Afghanistan, and the devastation of the Palestinians. A total restructuring of the world on egalitarian lines, including social ownership of property, decent standard of living for all, disciplining of wants and a fraternal feeling of co sharing, argued Dr. Lohia, were necessary for the maintenance of peace in each country and the world as a whole.

We, in India, are witnessing the tragedy of large scale displacement of the kisans and the triblas in resource rich States at the hands of the MNCs, in mad pursuit of mining for industrialization, in close alliance with the Central and State Governments. Since after independence, 60 million persons have been evacuated from their homes, and, according to authoritative sources, only one fifth among them have been rehabilitated. In respect of the dams on the Narmada river, a non violent struggle has been going on for the last 25 years, under Medha Patkar's leadership. The non- violent struggles launched by several groups to save the environment as Chilka Lake and Malkangiri hills in Orissa and the Koel Karo river in Jharkhand, the Silent Valley struggle in Kerala, Sunder Lal Bahuguna's long striving of saving displacements resulting from the Tehri Dam, the Chipko movement in Uttarakhand, the anti-WTO human chains organised by the Azadi Bachao Andolan, the Chhatra Yuva Sangharsh Vahini's agitation for the distribution of the vast properties of the Mahant of Bodh Gaya in 1976- 85, the non-violent agitations of the Bhils of western India under the leadership of Lohia's saintly disciple Mama Baleshwar Dayal and the protracted agitation against the compulsory use of the costly iodised salt by the veteran Gandhian Jagannathan are extensions of the teachings of Gandhi, Lohia and J.P. The governmental Gandhians, who have been suppressing these agitations by force, believe that it is the heretical Gandhians in the opposition, followers of J.P. and Lohia, who are their worst enemies, as they come from the same stock.

Lohia sought to modify the Gandhian way of austerity to provide a decent standard of living for all human beings, pleading that a life of sack cloth and ashes, in a world of plenty, would create internal conflicts in the minds of those who followed it. In a chapter, 'Materiality and Spirituality', in one of his books, he said that "freedom from gold through disciplining of wants... would require an effort of will almost as great as would achieve voluntarily a living death. Not only will all passions have to be subjugated and every single individual in society so trained as to control his mind as to desire, there would be no change and a vast stagnation would set in." He apprehended that such a system would degenerate and end in native feudalism or foreign conquest. Nor would it be possible in significant manner, both due to the world without and the world within. He alluded to Gandhi's strong advocacy of keeping the body clean, but felt that Gandhi did not take the body really into account, and sometimes, the cleanliness and the purity of the body were accompanied with its marginalization in practice. He was apprehensive that starving of the natural desires could create dissatisfaction which might propel thoughts of fulfilling them, thereby denigrating the spirituality of an individual who practiced it.

Gandhi's call for panchayats and gram swaraj appealed to Lohia, and he propounded a system of the Four Pillar State, Chaukhaba Raj, on that basis, with the village, the district, the state and the centre as its four pillars. The substance of power in this scheme remains with the village so that the individual finds a habitat to live in which he can control, while the ascending levels will have lesser powers successively. This scheme would take care of the demands of federalism and the division of powers between the states and the Centre. A World Government and a World Parliament of Lohia's dream would be the fifth tier of self governance The over centralization which came about in India after 1971 so that governmental and organisational power in the ruling Party the power in the was concentrated in the hands of the Prime Minister led to the rise of regional tensions. Together with regional economic imbalance created by the location of large industries in a few selected pockets, as was natural, it has strengthened fissiparous tendencies. Moreover, the present panchayati raj system is still dominated by bureaucrats. The state governments have been empowered to decide which subjects are to be entrusted to the panchayati raj institutions. Gandhi's view of party- less elections by consensus finds no place in it.. It is a matter of some satisfaction that women are being given 50 % reservation in the panchayat raj institutions, the credit for initiating which goes to the Chief Minister of Bihar, a disciple of Dr. Lohia.

But, Gandhi's picture of gram swaraj was incomplete with the decentralisation of developmental functions. He thought of the village as a self governing one, and Lohia's concept of the Four Pillar State thought in terms of Raj, that is, governance. Moreover, swadeshi, i.e. , economic self sufficiency in the village, together with full, decent employment for all, is a sine qua non of the scheme of gram swaraj. Lohia also insisted that a combination of political and economic decentralisation alone could give a fuller picture. But, one may not forget that Gandhi's constructive program included removal of unsociability and rural development, along with prohibition. Lohia stressed that unless the externment of women and backward castes, including the untouchables and other Scheduled Castes, from the society was ended, there could be no harmony in public life at any level, including the village. In respect of women, Lohia pleaded that man must consider woman as a human being like himself and treat her as his equal, Globalisation, however, has led to feminization in the developing countries where women are preferred as workers in industry, particularly entertainment and tourism, because they are considered the weaker sex and can be easily exploited physically and sexually.

Both Lohia and his ideal, Gandhi, were full of love for humanity. Lohia put pt in so many words by saying that in fighting injustice, there will be anger in one eye and tear in the other. This is the true spirit of satyagraha. But both went further, and this was one reason for their dispute with western civilization. They wanted man to live in harmony with nature, taking from it which was essentially needed, and then nourishing it as well. This is the model of sustainable growth. Gandhi emphasized that nature has everything to satisfy everyone's need, but not any one's greed. The west, on the other hand, sought to conquer nature, and exploit it to the maximum. Now that the threat of climate warming, melting of the glaciers, widening of the Ozone layer and slow extinction of some species have taught us to respect nature, there are people, and they are in positions of decision making, who love their profits more than humanity. One might refer to the fiasco in Copenhagen to point that out. It is a measure of Gandhi's wisdom that he made empathy with nature one of his cardinal points. Lohia also should be credited with having campaigned for cleaning the rivers and for formulating a policy for the Himalayas.

Gandhi had insisted on the use of the people's languages in all spheres of public life. Much before the linguistic redistribution of the country in mid 1950's, he had patterned the organisation of the Congress Party on that basis. Lohia alone, among his followers, made it a lifelong quest, though his campaigns for the removal of English from the administration and education were falsely characterized as Hindi zealotry. Unfortunately, globalization and information technology have been utilized by the Indian elite to bolster the use of English. The result of the policies of the succeeding Governments has been illiteracy of large masses of the people, poor quality of education and a system in which duality of schooling persists, strengthening the class- caste attributes of our society and the perpetuation of an anti- people administration whom even the decentralisation of power, to whatever extent it has come about, has failed to improve.

Lohia lived his later life with a deep regret. He had met Gandhi a day before the Mahatma's assassination. Gandhi had asked him to find time for a longer meeting the next evening which, however, never came. Lohia only continued to wonder what the great teacher wanted to tell him in respect of Lohia's role in free India. He, nevertheless, took upon himself the responsibility to extend the Master's message and continue with the latter's unfinished work. He had a complaint that the Mahatma was unlucky in his followers, a fact which visited him, too.

2

The Global Crisis: Gandhi and Lohia

Bhagwat Prasad Rath

A doubt arises ominous in the sky of human aspirations and dreams. Twenty-first century dawns with dire predictions of human race extinction, by a group of sober scientists whose credibility is beyond question. Way is there this fear in an age of dazzling technology and consumer boom? In the field of theories, confusion reigns. Science, the wizard, pours marvels from its never-exhausting bag. Neurology, Biotechnology, Nanotechnology: the churning of science ocean may yield nectar or world destroying poison.

Nature groans; temperature rises; climate goes hostile to survival; toxicity threatens the health of millions. Merrily the rich go on singing the pageans of the market piling goods sky-high. Again and again, the tides of the sea of poverty futilely dash against their rocks of growing fabulous wealth. The human race has only 50:50 chance of survival declares David Ross, British Royal Astronomer. Lord May, David King and Diamond: all hard realists prominent in the field of science warn that global collapse is a real possibility. Every social and eco-system, either nourished or ravaged by centuries of human effort is facing the grave risk of collapse.Craig Venter of J.C.V. Science Foundation blames the human gene for future human extinction. Richard Dawkins of Oxford University puts his finger on the pulse when he says that a murderer or a rapist has either a defective brain or a faulty upbringing, the second one is more likely in most cases in the present age."What we lack is political will" declares Paul Davies, a physicist.

Prophetically declares Royal Society President Martin Rees, ".....The decisions that we make, individually or collectively, will determine whether the outcomes of 21st century science are benign or devastating."

Gandhi and Lohia are precisely those thinkers whose ideas, backed by strong political wills, will save human civilization from sure collapse. The two greatest evils that rock human society can be pinpointed in terms of the famed humanist psychologist Erich From. In his book "Man Makes Himself." From describes the marketing-oriented character of the modern man thus "In our time the marketing orientation has been growing rapidly together with the development of a new market that is a phenomenon of the last decades, the personality market." Now we have two markets, the commodity market and the personality market. In a survey conducted in a Girls High School in the U.S, 93% girls declared their first hobby as shopping. Because of the existence of the personality market, many are coerced to wear a pleasant mask along with the manipulated personality. This ubiquitous marketing orientation has created extremely selfish men and selfish nations and has legitimized cut-throat competitions.

As science scales new heights, surveillance measures gain better precision, thus making the all knowing big brother of 1984 a reality. The corporations utilize all conceivable methods to collect data about human beings as consumers. Of late, Neurology, too, has contributed to the erosions of human privacy. Bright-house, previously an advertising firm, with the collaboration of Emory University, is utilizing MRI (Magnetic Resonance Imaging) techniques to tap the pre-dispositions of the limbic brain and thus to influence the unconscious mind.

Greed, envy, arrogance: all the vices decried by different religions of the world are utilized to enhance the marketing potential sky-high. Castes based on consumer hierarchy make modern society an unfeeling exploiting one. As community solidarity gets gradually replaced by crass individualism, Narcissistic tendencies grow and even the family gets undermined by the selfish market-made man or woman. Children suffer as a result. Anti-socials proliferate, Mental illnesses double in every third decade. The one-dimensional man or the cheerful robot is the ultimate outcome of the market oriented personality. No wonder, alienation haunts the most sensitive spirits of the modern society. When it becomes unbearable, they lose their sanity.

The second evil that plagues human society, both in the past and the present, is the military-orientation of character. This character which develops the trait of either a Faraday on a Robinson Crusoe knows obedience or command as the greatest virtues of human beings. Such people become either ruthless dictators or slaves. They become unfit as enlightened citizens for whom human rights are the greatest values. No wonder many of them join communal organizations, hawking violence and hatred, wrecking societies and countries. People who prefer a violent revolution are not aware that such revolutionaries develop sick personalities and after coming to power become cruel and devourers of the civic rights of anyone who dares to differ. Every violent revolution aborts all future revolutions for a generation as no one who differs with the leader is given a chance to live. Mao's theory of permanent revolution is the first casualty in every violet revolution. That hatred and violent are human-personality-endangering vices comes out in the recent research findings of the brain-scientists.

"The core point of convergence between the Buddhist and Psychological perspectives is that 'hostility', which is viewed in the West as a character or personality, trait, is considered to be destructive to one's health. Impulsive chronic violence is also considered to be dysfunctional and is classified as pathological, (Davidson, Putnam & Larson 2000.)

(An extract from an article ("*Buddhist & Psychological Perspective on Emotion and Well Being*" written jointly by Paul Ekman (University of California, San Fransisco), R.J. Davidoson (University of Wisconsin, Madison), Mathew Ricard (Budhist scholar). B.A. Wallace (S.B. Institute for conscientiousness Studies. Santa Barbara, California).

Marx's materialism ignored the matter that has the greatest influence on human personality, the grey matter preserved in the human brain. No change in external circumstances can influence the racist or the schizophrenic who weaves his own illusive world. Marx's followers dreaming of a better world and ready to sacrifice everything for their noble cause ultimately became victims of the defective neural paths that crisscross their brains. Neither Polpot nor Stalin, or the Tibet-ravishing Mao are aberrations of communist revolutions. The military orientation of personality often does grievous injury to society.

The military and the marketing-oriented characters become doubly dangerous when they are reinforced by each other. The US has proved to be the greatest wrecker of peace in the 20th century. It is the leading terrorist country in the world callously murdering millions in other countries to safeguard the profits of its exploiting big corporations. The industry-military complex of the US is the greatest violator of human rights not only in America but also in remote areas of the world. Boosting the murderous activities of dictators like Suharto of Indonesia and Pinochet of chile, the US has proved the greatest evil power of the modern age. It maintains training centers to demonize military officers of the Latin American countries. Its prisons are inhuman institutions. The US uses human rights with non-chalant hypocrisy to invade and occupy resource-rich countries like Iraq. America's war expenses in Iraq are expected to reach trillions in near future. The US spends fabulous amounts on the military.

As spoken by the journalist Thomas Friedan, "For globalization of the world America can't be afraid to act like the almighty superpower that it is. The hidden hand market will never work without the hidden fist." America spends far more than the combination of the next fifteen nations who are the largest spenders for defence. Every day the US spends about 75,000 million rupees on the military. Rs.8,000 million everyday will suffice to banish hunger from the face of the earth. More than half of the US's Federal Discretionary Budget is spent for the military. The US is the worst among the developed countries in the field of child mortality as in New York. "During 45 years of the cold war with the Soviet union, the US intervened more than 200 times militarily in foreign countries" (ADDICTED TO WAR by J. Andreas). Gandhi and Lohia are among the leading thinkers whose ideas can save the world from the grave crisis threatening modernity.

Gandhi's stress on the principle of APARIGRAHA (Reducing human wants to the minimum) is the only remedy against the marketing orientation. Lohia, too, led a life of APARIGRAHA though APARIGRAHA was not a creed for him. He had no property worth its name in life. His death was equally unostentatious, as per his wish. An electric oven burnt his dead body without any paraphernalia accompanying it either before or after its disposal.

The age-old values of APARIGRAHA and ASTEYA (Giving the society its due, before any individual enjoys wealth) which is wrongly translated as non-stealing, constitute the bedrock of any socialist society. Communism et its demise in almost all the red countries only because these two values were given a goodbye in them. Today, with the environment going toxic, the present civilization can save itself only by giving importance to these two values. The west which seems to be genetically or socially programmed to welcome strife and prodigality must change its course; otherwise dire disaster awaits humanity.

Gandhi and Lohia were both votaries of non-violent revolutions. Gandhi's discovery of Satyagraha was the greatest gift to the present war and slaughter-prone humanity. By making truth and non-violence an inseparable pair, Gandhi made the military irrelevant for a happiness-seeking world society.

Today's globalization slogan has been devised to boost the market. As spoken by Prof. J.K. Galbraith, "Globalization is not a serious concept. We have invented it to disseminate our politics of economic entry into other countries."

Unfortunately even our leftist friends in India have neither lost their fascination for industrialization leading to the growth of the market nor the military's dominance in either national or revolutionary activities. Marx's legacy seems to be much eloquent in both the fields as it was a product of nineteenth century Europe, the progeny of both a war-loving ancient Yehova land and the warrior-mentality-dominated Hellenist Greece. Europe's climate of scarcity barely gave it scope to welcome a leisurely quality-rich life of voluntary poverty except amongst a section of religious people. The Yogic tradition in India is unique in the world in making minds truly free and compassionate without any help of magic, ritual or god. Three important religious streams of India are children of the Yogic culture. They are Buddhism, Jainism and the Yogic Hindu groups. From ancient days when God and Satan occupied the western mind, dichotomies ruled the west's realms of culture. Separation of the sacred and the secular, the Appollonian and the Dionysian, truth and values led the west to great heights of science-based material splendor, combined with conspicuous moral depravity and the rise of monstrous organizations like the TNCs. In the field of methodology, science's amoral stance in the cause of truth, paid dividends, but, in another field, the choice of areas of scientific research were decided by the employers of scientists who merrily fattened themselves on the vices like greed and hate. Separation of the sacred and the secular robed the secular field of the vital energy associated with primal emotions. The sacred utilizing the immense potentiality of basic emotions irrigated the realm of fanaticism. In every religion, fanatics outnumbered the moderates. In India the emotions and concepts moved together, the sacred and the secular shook hands in the field of values.

In the fertile grounds, of miracles magic and rituals, many world religions (including Hinduism) had their birth and growth. Faith, rather than rationality, guides the Semitic religions as well as Hinduism. Only Buddhism and Jainism are atheistic religions based on rationality. Unfortunately these two religions also were mostly male-dominated and accepted the role of enlightened souls as revered Gurus. Only the Pre-Vedic Anwikshiki society (read Koutilya), combining the world views and practices of Yoga, Samkhya and Lokayata was free from these defects. Rationality, avoidance of negative emotions and nurturance of positive emotions, distinguish this society from all others, primitive and modern. Religion and ideology: both matured to a happy marriage in Anwikshiki society. Anwikshki society was women-centric and 'Maitri' towards all living creatures was its core-value. 'Maitri' led to the culturing of values like truth, asetya, aparigraha and compassion.

Indigenous societies, whose limited violence and caring-sharing values provide hope for the thinkers dreaming of a better society, nurture a number of superstitions because of their devotion to magic and ritual. Knowledge of such non-competitive egalitarian indigenous societies where superstitions based on Totem and Taboo prevail, does not serve the cause of genuine democratic socialism, based on rationality and empathy. Einstein was impressed by the peaceful and egalitarian Pueblo Indians; Harry Magdoff became eloquent in narrating the egalitarian values of pre-Columbian Americans. The existence of such societies proves that human nature yields to nurture to a great extent.

With confidence, one can assert that unless we accept the values of ASTEYA and APARIGRAHA, the earth cannot be saved from the greed of an ever-expanding consumerist society. Similarly, unless truth and non violence are combined, no democratic society can come into being. These four values are enough to banish want and consumerism to the dustbins of history.

Gandhi's trusteeship theory which won the loyalty of Lohia also, is fully based on the principle of ASTEYA. ASTEYA reaches great heights when combined with APARIGRAHA. Gandhi did not live long enough to subject his trusteeship theory to the rigours of practicality and its universal application. Lohia, pre-occupied as he was with a defective polity, too, could only pay lip service to the theory of Trustee-ship. This theory's success depends on the cultural level of the people and the proper social structures of different societies. Marx's grand ideas lost relevance when greedy and paranoid people became rulers, Independent India imitated the West and relegated Gandhi to the pedestals of the backrooms.

Time is fast running out. The contented class and its Frankensteins, the TNC's complacently strive to undermine age-old values and demolish the old cultural contours. Either we become wiser or we succumb to Thanatos (Death wish). Promotion of consumerist culture and military culture and institutions based on them are producing unhealthy human beings who are unfit for a Gandhian socialist society. Anthropology and brain science in the present state of society, applied wisely, are capable of guiding us in the right direction. Yogic practices and Buddhist disciplines which have developed through millenniums give us hope that both the conscious and unconscious parts of the human mind can be influenced to build a character which is virtuous by almost all humanist standards. Such a character accepts ecological and Gandhian socialistic principles. Marxism which is protean in its spread has nurtured a type of social change based on non-violent struggles, given popularity by William Morris. This variety of Marxism and the ecologically-sound variety of Marxism as propagated by J.B. Foster, of Monthly Review fame, can easily blend with Gandhian socialism and Buddhist humanism.

Simply wishing a new society and painting it with broad strokes of brush is not enough. Constant debates must take place about the cultural and institutional aspects of this society and the way to implement them. Many of the Europe and America-based theories including the present trend, Post-Modernism, ignore the plight of the Third world. Gandhi and Lohia are original thinkers who blazed new trails for humanity. J.P. and M.N. Roy are two others thinkers who cannot be ignored in the Indian context. Decentralization of power which materializes in the form of Gram-Swaraj of Gandhi was equally emphasized by Lohia, J.P., and Roy. The Green Party of Germany also gave the central place in its manifesto to this concept. A fuller discussion of this matter waits in the corridors of history. Utopias, having birth in the West, have created a scare among social thinkers. To set at rest their misgivings regarding utopias turning totalitarian, every such social scheme must make the Yogic four values and scientific rationalism (Buddha was a votary of it) the bed rock of such societies. Anthropology, sociology and Psychology (Particularly modern brain science and Buddhist Yogic practices) have the great potential to guide us in preparing a good scheme. Scientists of the environment institute of Stockholm have done a great job by pinpointing the global problems and the proposed remedy. J.B. Foster has made a commendable study of Marxism Ecology. We have to move further along the same road. People who claim the legacy of Gandhi and Lohia are particularly in favorable positions to examine the scheme and make corrections. The West's mainstream understanding of the Third World may not satisfy original thinkers of the East. After the publication of the book "Orientalism" of Edward Said, expression of such doubts will not be misunderstood even in the West. There is a side stream in the West which is mostly fed by Christian values. This stream is extremely valuable for every Eastern thinker. Gandhi used the ideas of the few great thinkers of the West fruitfully. We cannot ignore many of the great thinkers of the west as our legacy is global at present. Indians have the unique legacy of the Buddha and Gandhi. They should have a debate with humanist and socialist thinkers of the west to prepare a blue-print for a sustainable and happy society.

Gandhi and Lohia were against caste violence. Gandhi devoted a lot of his time to Dalit Upliftment. Lohia defied caste hierarchy to give justice to the lower oppressed classes. Ambedkar fought all his life to abolish caste oppression. We are heirs to the great legacies of Gandhi and Ambedkar. Dalit intellectual Nagraj in his famous book "The Flaming Feet" explains how the two liberators of humanity complement each other. The Buddhist stream of thought had tremendous influence on the people of Asia. Today, almost all the leading intellectuals in the world appreciate the Buddha. It was to the credit of Ambedkar that he contributed a lot to the revival of Buddha's thoughts in India. In our attempt to build a better world society, we have to lay under toll all these great legacies of the East and the West as well as those of Arabia as pointed out by the best humanist Islamic thinkers of the whole world.

REFERENCES

1. J.B. Foster, Global Ecology and the Common Good, Monthly Review, Feb. 1995.
2. Varva Burstyn, (2005). The New Imperial Order, Foretold *Socialist Register,* p. 7.
3. Albert Einstein (1988). Ideas and Opinions – Ediiton , Compulsory service (p.107). The Military Mentality (p.132).

3

Bose, Gandhi and Ambedkar: Their Ideology

K. Raghu Ram Reddy & A. Hariprasad

Subhas Chandra Bose popularly called "Netaji" was primarily an uncompromising and relentless fighter for India's Freedom. He is one of the political lumanaries in the galaxy of Indian leaders who fought for the emancipation of our motherland from the yoke of alien masters. He was the most controversial and colorful figure, in fact, a legendary one in India's struggle for Independence.

Dr.B.R. Ambedkar, the champion of down trodden and the crusader of social equality held a prominent position among the twentieth century leaders of India. He realized that distortion of religion and misinterpretation of history and culture did more harm to Indian social life than foreign invasions and domination of centuries. Ambedkar took upon himself the taste of fighting for religious, social and economic equality in the Indian society.

Mohandas Karamchand Gandhi, the 'Father of the Nation' and the 'Architect of modern India' respectfully, addressed and remembered as Mahatma, was born on the cross-roads of our history and gave it a purposeful direction .He made his mark as protester, social worker, reformer, thinker and as the liberator. The political guise in which he appeared before the world he did not own. He was religious, humanist and the "practical idealist". He accepted life in all its comprehensiveness.

In this paper we made an attempt to compare and contrast the ideologies of Subhas Chandra Bose, Baba Saheb Ambedkar and Mohandas Karamchand Gandhi, the three important leaders of the Indian National Movement or Indian Freedom Struggle.

Subhas Chandra Bose was one among the few who had joined Indian National Congress but did not accept Gandhism as philosophy. He, like M. Tayyebula considered Gandhi's philosophy as "a vague philosophy". "A religious credo", "a beautiful, beautiful, beautiful vision" and "a religious ideal" but not something which can be called politics. Instead C.R. Das attracted Subhas Bose. The brilliant academic record of Bose attracted C.R. Das. Bose participated in non-cooperation movement led by Gandhiji, but severely criticized for its suspension. Bose was attracted to the Swaraj Party formed by C.R. Das. He considered Swaraj Party as more radical. After the death of C.R. Das Bose become closer to Jawaharlal Nehru. Both of them were instrumental in passing the resolution for complete independence. However, Bose and Nehru parted the ways after some time. Bose entertained left nationalist ideology, he organized the youth and workers of India. Bose was unhappy with the non aggressive attitude of Gandhi in the "Round Table Conference of 1930". Bose considered Gandhi as an old useless piece of furniture. He realised that he was undermined in the congress party. Nehru also did not stand with him. So he resigned to the congress party and founded the Forward Block. He formed an association called Azad Hind League in Berlin. He reached Japan in 1943 and joined I.N.A. whose leader was Rash Behari. His life came to a mysterious end on August 18th 1945.

Netaji was a fire brand patriot and a progressive militant nationalist. He was influenced by Mazzini and Garibaldi who unified Italy. He was also influenced by George Washington, Tilak and Arabindo. Bose was a liberal religious man. For him, mother and motherland are superior to Heaven. He deified the nation. He wanted to make any kind of sacrifice to liberate his mother land. He asked the people also to sacrifice. He desired that every nation must establish its identity in the community of nations. He considered INA as a strong vehicle to fight the British and get independence. Bose always called for selfless sacrifice at the altar of a nation that's why he said "Give me blood I will give you freedom". Bose believed that every nation needs a political ideology of its own reflecting its own culture and indigenous solution. He developed the ideology of samyavada which was a synthesis of both fascism and communism. However he rejected the anti spiritual, atheistic and materialistic aspects of communism. He also condemned narrow, selfish, arrogant and racist aspects of fascism. He was a socialist nationalist and democratic socialist. He favoured a strong government which only could solve India's problems. He wanted one party dictatorship for some time with military discipline. He rejected parliamentary democracy. He had great pride in Indian culture and in its heritage. He wanted to build a country with self reliance.

Bose was both a political activist and visionary. He was a unique crusader for Swaraj, he was a militant nationalist. He championed the cause of down trodden and destitudes of the society. His book the "Indian Struggle" reflects his political ideas and goals. Complete independence was his political goal. He wanted to make Indian people moral, honest and self sacrifice. He was sorry to see the disappearance of ancient principles like equality, fraternity and the rise of capitalists and landlords who joined the Britishers. Fight against the imperialism was another political goal of Subas Chandra Bose. His nationalism was progressive and democratic but never aggressive. Bose adopted the techniques of uncompromising revolt, extremism to the extent of sacrificing one's life in the fight against British imperialism. He believed in the concept of end justify the means. For Bose end was important. Bose had a strong faith in the principle of extremism. He criticized Gandhi's non violence- as an extremely soft and the legacy of mendicant policy of the moderates. He wanted to attack the British imperialist army from outside and did not see any wrong in taking the help of outside powers. He thought that Gandhiji could never change the heart of British government through prayer and appeal. He favoured socialist measures to bring about equality, prosperity in Indian society.

Netaji and Gandhi

Netaji believed in a strong courageous, brave India and the might of the sword. Gandhi believed in truth and non-violence and the might of soul. But both worked for the liberation of the mother land. Netaji was a fervent nationalist.

Gandhiji was a reluctant nationalist. Bose did not like Gandhi's idea of compromise and co-operation. In 1939 Netaji was the president of Indian National Congress and asked the Britishers to leave the country within six months. Gandhi also toed the line of Netaji with his 1942 Quit India Movement when he gave his thunderous call for "do or die". Bose criticized Gandhi's non-violent Satyagraha as a technique to arouse public opinion but certainly not to make India free. He argued that non-violence should be supplemented by diplomacy and international propaganda. Necessary swords must be raised against the British rule, because Britishers ruled Indians through sword. Gandhi suggested for tolerance. Bose stood for sharp reaction. Bose believed in force to dislodge the alien rulers from Indian soil. Bose was a critic of Gandhi's ideas of Charka and Trusteeship. Bose believed in socialist measures to abolish landlordism, capitalism and stood for planned development to remove poverty and illiteracy. Bose was influenced by the doctrine of scientific socialism of Karl Marx. He was impressed by the success of Soviet Russia. However, Bose did not become a communist. He did not accept the anti religious doctrine of Marx and proletariat dictatorship. The culture, tradition and heritage of India were not conducive for the adoption of soviet communism. He was against class war. Bose devised a new type of communism which may be called Indian socialism. Bose was not a fascist also, but he was impressed with the performance of fascism in unifying Germany and Italy. He opposed Victorian democracy in U.K. and advocated single party dictatorship. His socialism was a synthesis of communism and fascism. Bose believed that Swaraj or complete independence should be the primary objective of each nation. As a socialist Bose gave primacy to the socio-economic freedom. Without a democratic society political democracy will be weak. Democratic society will be possible only when social freedom is guaranteed for all. This implies the abolition of privileges based upon birth, caste and creed. Social equality will pave the way for social freedom. Bose also emphasized economic liberty which means freedom from poverty, hunger and starvation. To solve these problems he argued economic equality must be established by abolishing landlordism and capitalism by socializing the system of agricultural and industrial production through planning. Bose's concept of freedom was comprehensive which included all sections of the Indian society. He supported the introduction of fundamental rights in the Indian constitution favoured universal adult franchise and stood for an independent federal republic. His concept of Swaraj and freedom were both nationalist and socialist in character.

Gandhi wanted to eliminate all kinds of economic inequalities, exploitation and poverty through trusteeship. He believed that political independence will be of no use without economic independence. He preferred a limited state and wanted the villages to be self sufficient republics. He opposed big industries which will displace man power .He preffered cottage industries. Netaji prefferred one party rule. Gandhi prefferred party less rule .Gandhi was against fascism, nazism and communism.

Netaji was not against religion but opposed mixing religion with politics. Gandhi preferred mixing religion and politics but opposed state patronizing any particular religion. Netaji did not separately fight for the emancipation of downtrodden sections including women. His idea was that independence will automatically take care of their interests including women.

Ambedkar and Gandhi

Ambedkar was the leader of Untouchables. He worked for their emanpicition throughout his life. He considered *Manusmruti* responsible for the sufferings of Untouchables in India. Hence he has burnt it in 1927. He waited for change among Hinduss and acceptance of Untouchables on par with them. Since there was no sign of change among Hinduss he took to Buddhism and conveyed the message of equality, brotherhood and peace to the whole world.

Gandhi and Ambedkar both rejected formal Democracy as being inadequate as well as harmful, Gandhi favored decentralized democratic setup but Ambedkar showed his preference for what he called social democracy. However, both came down to accept formal democracy as being a practical proposition. Gandhi was ready to grant all the necessary civic rights to the untouchables but Ambedkar insisted upon autonomous political status of the Untouchables, and therefore, demanded separate electorate.

Gandhi was firm in his stand that the problems of the untouchables were to be tackled within the fold of Hinduism and the Hindu social order lest double split implied in Ambedkar's demand for separate electorates render the Hindu social order a dead entity. He insisted that the evils of Hindu social order must be removed so that the untouchables may enjoy a life of dignity.

Ambedkar believed in party system and established a political party known as Republican Party of India with the aim of providing a vehicle for untouchables to fight for their rights. Both Gandhi and Ambedkar believed in peaceful methods to achieve the objective of emancipation of untouchables. Gandhi gave more importance to freedom for India which will be equally enjoyed by untouchables also. Ambedkar gave more importance to emancipation and freedom of untouchables.

REFERENCES

1. R.C.Gupta, *Great Political Thinkers East and West,* Lakshmi Narain Agarwal, Agra, 2006
2. Ian Adams and R.W.Dyson, *Fifty Great Political Thinkers,* Rout ledge, London and New York, 2004
3. Sridhar Charan Sahoo, *Subhash Chandra Bose (Political Philosophy),* APH Publishing Corporation, New Delhi, 1997.
4. K.N.Kadam, *Dr. B.R. Ambedkar, the Emancipator of the oppressed, A Centenary Commemoration Volume,* (Ed.), popularprakasham, Bombay, 1993
5. Anthony J.Parel, (ed.), *Gandhi's, Freedom. and Self-Rule,* vistaar publications, New Delhi, 2002
6. Rameshray Ray, *Gandhi and Ambedkar, A Study in Contrast,* SHIPRA Publications, Delhi, 2006.
7. N.Jaya Palan, *Indian Political Thinkers, Modern Indian Political Thought,* Atlantic Publishers, Delhi, 2003
8. Vishnoo Bhagwan, *Indian Political Thinkers,* Atma Ram and Sons, Delhi, Lucknow, 2006
9. Saila Kumar Ghosh, *Colonial Modernization and Gandhi,* Ajith Kumar for PAPYRUS, Kolkata, 2008
10. Pradeep Bose *Subhash Chandra Bose and India Today A New Tryst with Destiny?* Deep and Deep Publication, New Delhi, 1999.

4

Confronting Gandhi: Ambedkar's Views on Future Religion of the Hindus

Ch.Y Sudhakar

Nothing can be bitter than the experience of Untouchability. The Hindu religion is blind for this curse of evil. Never, they dreamed to hear the outcry against such an inhuman practice. Baba Saheb Bhimrao Ambedkar is the first person to fight against this kind of ethical terror. As a school boy, when he was not allowed to share a common drink with that of a society to which he belonged he started his resistance. His life became a continuous fight against the Hindu's religion putting them to rethink of their age old practices with disbelief. If belief and blind adherence to the prescribed authority is the way of goodness, well Ambedkar is bad enough to challenge those authorities and dare to author the Indian constitution liberating millions of men from their hereditary ill treatment. During the second round table conference the British government came out with a suggestion that the minority's interests shall be protected with the creation of separate communal constituencies especially reserved for them. Among them the name of the depressed (dalits) classes also shall be included because of their pitiable status of untouchability. If this is not acceptable there appeared to be a stalemate for the Indians in drafting a constitution for a responsible and self-ruling government. Gandhi opposed for the creation of any such constitutional measures in the name of the special communal constituencies for the dalits as they became a part of the Hindu religion but not a separate minority group like that of the Muslims and Sikhs. Gandhi spoke in the conference

"I do not mind Untouchables, if they so desire, being converted to Islam or Christianity. I should tolerate that, but I cannot possibly tolerate for what is in store for Hindu's if there are two divisions set forth in the villages. Those who speak of the political rights of Untouchables do not know their India , do not know how Indian society is to-day constructed , and therefore I want to say with all the emphasis that I can command that if I was the only person to resist this thing I would resist it with my life. [1]

The above statement of M.K. Gandhi shows how Gandhi and congress party denied giving any privileges and special rights to the depressed classes. What Gandhi told cannot be taken in any adverse sense, but shall be considered in a context of the division and separation that may cause to the depressed classes with any such special constituencies which were proposed by the British government. With bitter experiences of the untouchability Ambedkar could not yield to the demands of Gandhi. Finally Gandhi went on hunger strike as a policy of his agitation and finally resisted Ambedkar and British government's designs for the separate Electoral constituencies. Ambedkar being a sincere and sophisticated humanitarian could respond with sympathy to the demands of Gandhi and made him to give up his hunger strike. As a matter of reciprocation Gandhi accepted for the representation of the Dalits or the depressed classes in the government with adequate general and common constituencies. This shows the way how the depressed classes of India were liberated and saved from the clutches of senseless orthodoxy. This marked the end of social hegemony of certain sections within Indian society in the name of Hindu religious code of conduct given by Manu.

Ambedkar's fight with untouchability starts with a quest to find the very origins of Caste system of the Hindu Religion. Ambedkar is known for his famous papers Castes in India and Annihilation of Caste. He felt very annoying not only the condition of Untouchability but also the very system of caste. He wrote in his paper Castes in India that the caste problem is a vast one; both theoretically and practically. Practically it is an institution that portends tremendous consequences.

It is a local problem, but one capable of much wider mischief, for as long as caste in India does exist, Hindus will hardly intermarry or have any social intercourse with outsiders; and if Hindus migrate to other regions on earth, Indian caste would become a world problem. [2]

Ambedkar did not find any proper reason in the division based on caste. Ambedkar says that it is not the division of labor as it was boasted by the Hindu Hierarchy. He says that it is the division of the laborers. He did not feel satisfied with the then existing caste theories. He tried to examine all these theories with utmost attention and finally says that they failed to represent properly in a comprehensive manner. In an elaborate observation Ambedkar tries to find out the roots of the caste system. But he could trace three customs in practice closely related to the caste problem. With the observation of these three practices namely Sati, Enforced Widowhood and Child Marriage, we can determine the distance of one caste from the principal caste that of the Brahmins. People used to believe them as virtues. But regarding the origin and development of castes, Ambedkar writes the following lines.

> I said that the Brahmin class first raised the structure of caste by the help of those three customs in question.[3]

Caste in the singular number is an unreality. Castes exist only in the plural number.[4] There is no such thing as a caste. There are always castes.[5] While making themselves into a caste, the Brahmins, by virtue of this, created non-Brahmin caste; or to express it in my own way,

> While closing themselves in, they closed others out.[6]

The logic of Hindu caste system shows that it is a mechanism that brings into existence, the system of caste or the castes. In this process no caste allows to go free without punishment of its offenders. Expulsion becomes this punishment Thus when a courageous person violates the law, he will be excommunicated and all such persons will be encouraged to form a new caste. Such is the Hindu Psychology.[7]

The punishment for the offender of the law or for any offence against the law will not take into consideration the actual offence and its nature. All offenders will fall into one category. When these people are encouraged to form a new caste, there will be the emergence of new castes. From all the above observations we can see that Caste is not a single entity. It can be observed as the system of operation. And in that sense both Untouchability and Caste operate together and become the reflection of the other. In this respect Ambedkar questions the very authenticity of the Indians fighting for their freedom; it happened like that while Gandhi is trying to eradicate untouchability, the effects appeared to be very meager and the depressed classes do not feel satisfied to take part in the freedom struggle. Yet in his address Ambedkar reflects the very wish to join the freedom struggle against the British Imperialists. But only with one condition, if the independence to India is guaranteed there shall be some protection for the depressed classes. That protection comes from the very constitutional measures which he felt will be very perfect. In this respect he argued for the inclusion of Untouchability as a punishable crime. And in that process Ambedkar came out with a final clause to be included in the constitution that any kind of discrimination will become punishable.

We cannot consider Ambedkar's ideas as mere the feelings due to phobia. Ambedkar quotes so many examples. They are:

1. The rules of conduct imposed on Balais of Maharashtra.
2. The Kairthe incident of Gujarat.
3. The Zenu incident of Ahmedabad District
4. Chakwara incident in Jaipur State.[8]

The rules of conduct imposed on Balais of Maharashtra

This incident was reported in the Times of India of 4th January 1928. this incident had taken place in the Indore district of Indore State. The caste group that came under the imposed conduct for the depressed classes were the Balais. It was informed to them by the forward and high castes of that region that if they wanted to live with them they shall follow the following rules.

1. Balais must not wear dhotis with colored or fancy borders.
2. They must not wear gold-lace –bordered pugrees.
3. They must convey intimation of the death of any Hindu to relatives of the deceased–no matter how far away these relatives may be living.
4. In all the Hindu marriages, Balais must play music before the processions and during the marriage.

5. Balais women must not wear gold or silver ornaments; they must not wear fancy gowns or jackets.
6. Balais women must attend all cases of confinement of Hindu women.
7. Balais must render services without demanding remuneration and must accept whatever a Hindu is pleased to give.

They did not agree to oblige and as a result the Balais were persecuted with social boycott by the villagers of that region and finally they were forced to migrate to other regions. Even though petitions were filed against such boycotts nothing had taken any shape to help them. And finally the migration took place. [9]

The Kavitha incident of Gujarat

This incident took place in Gujarat. Here the depressed class children were ordered not to study in the common village schools. These schools were actually maintained by the government. They too met the same consequences even though they aspired for the civil rights.

The Zenu incident of Ahmedabad District

This incident also took place in the state of Gujarat again. In Nov. 1935 some untouchable women of well –to- do families started to fetch water in metal pots. This annoyed the high castes and simply in return was assaulted.

Chakwara incident in Jaipur State

An Untouchable of Chakwara village in Jaipur state returned from a pilgrimage and wanted to treat his guests with an arranged dinner who were also happened to be the other untouchables. The host desired to treat the guests with a good meal which contained ghee among those served. ... the Hindus having known this, armed with lathis in hundred in number. attacked the dinner party.

Such were the cases of the lives of the untouchables before the time of independence. For these people there cannot be any rescue as these practices have the social acceptance and were supported by false interpretation of the texts often whose originality is in question. Untouchability cannot be treated without an understanding of the Caste system. That is what actually was done by Ambedkar. In his pursuit of this effect, Ambedkar in his

Book Annihilation of Caste published his ideas regarding the Hindu society and religion. Ambedkar's main idea is to clear from the concept of caste, the sentiment it carries with itself. Sentiment must be outlawed from the domain of science and things should be judged from an objective standpoint.[10]

Ambedkar cites so many examples of the atrocities of untouchability. From the above examples we observe that sentiment in reality regarding the conduct of these depressed class people. Ambedkar feels very much annoyed and felt the desperation regarding the religious ideas of the Hindus. He writes

> I have no hesitation in saying that if the Mohammedan has been cruel the Hindu has been mean and meanness is worse than that cruelty.[11]

Having stated all the above four incidents, Ambedkar puts forward the following questions.

1. Are you fit for political power even though you do not allow a large class of your own country men like the untouchables to use public schools?
2. Are you fit for political power even though you do not allow them the use of public wells?
3. Are you fit for political power even though you do not allow them the use of public streets?
4. Are you fit for political power even though you do not allow them to wear what apparel and ornaments they like?
5. Are you fit for political power even though you do not allow them to eat any food they like? [12]

Ambedkar strongly believed that social changes and reformations will precede the political revolutions. And Ambedkar finds religion as the source of power in India. Ambedkar did not consider the supportive arguments of the casteists. He questioned and disproved their arguments. In his "Who were the shudras" he comes across the different theories and finally concludes that once upon a time shudras were also given the right to perform sacrificial rights but later they were denied. His profound familiarity with the Indian legendary literature like Puranas and the Vedic lore makes Ambedkar an unquestioned authority over the Hindu affair. He finally comes to define an ideal society and some prescription to reform the Hindus and the Hindu society. His prescription contained the following ideas. In his Chapter XIV of Annihilation of Caste, Ambedkar says that his ideal society will be society based on Liberty, Equality, and Fraternity.[13]

Ambedkar describes the characteristics of an Ideal society.

1. An ideal society shall be a mobile society.
2. An ideal society contains communication channels for communicating the changes taking place in one part to the other parts.
3. There will be many interests which are consciously communicated and shared.
4. There will be varied and free points of contact with other modes of association. This he calls it as the social Endosmosis.

The ideas of Chaturvarnya are disliked by Ambedkar. He says that the Laws of Manu are the infamous laws. Any kind of injustice in the world was far behind the evil structures of Manu. The social revolutions spread all over the world where as they were totally absent from the Indians. For this Ambedkar sees the social structure as the cause. The Chaturvarnya system had disabled and crippled all the weaker sections of the people of India. Without arms they could not rebel. But arms were made unavailable and even though became available the expertise required was not at all available with the Indians because of the Manu smrithi which denied any kind of state craft or warfare known to the Indians. Either they have remained as plough men are denied even to be plough men. They had no ability to resist violently and because of this every one came and sat over them. Chaturvarnya makes them crippled of education. Thought becomes impossible and salvation in that process becomes impossible. They were reconciled with eternal servitude because of this. This servitude they had accepted as their fate. It became an inescapable fate for them.. Even though in Europe also the exploitation of the weak existed it could not be of this magnitude. And it is among the Hindus this exploitation solidified. In the case of the Europeans, there existed freedom to military education which provided them with the military weapons to use. In the case of politics the political freedom brought them over with the political weaponry. And in the case of morals, education equipped them with the moral instruments. In the Indian chaturvarnya system these weapons were denied. There can not be any moral degradation than this chaturvarnya system. Ambedkar finds the only period of the Mauryan when these were available to the masses of India when freedom, greatness and glory shined over the history of Indians. During this period caste was annihilated and shudras came into power and became the rulers of India.

Regarding the period of the Chaturvarnya system, Ambedkar traces their history to be as ancient as of that of the Vedas. All the history of the Indians is fully packed with the strife between two castes one that of the Kings and second that of the Brahmins. Both of them were irresponsible towards these masses. Both were successful at different periods. But none of them could give a solace to the masses. Sometimes they prayed to god the almighty. Despite of this past, Ambedkar fails to understand why the Indians preferred the chaturvarnya system. Ambedkar finds no reason to accept this chaturvarnya system to be a suitable model[14].

Ambedkar finds two specific points in the attitude of the Indians towards caste system. Their attitude to the problem of caste is not merely an attitude of neutrality, but is an attitude of armed neutrality. A major section of the Indian society is not only neutral but they do not feel peculiarity of the caste system. These people try to show the different stratifications of the Muslims as well as that of the Sikhs to support their attitude.[15]

Ambedkar did not feel satisfied with the leaders like S. Radhakrishnan. Ambedkar could not accept their arguments. Ambedkar thinks of the following questions.

1. How to bring about the reform of thc Hindu social order?
2. How to abolish caste?

Ambedkar finally comes out to prescribe the following changes. In that process Ambedkar gives five cardinal points as a solution. They are:

1. There should be one and only one standard book of Hindu Religion, acceptable to all Hindus and recognized by all Hindus. This involves the ban of all other books like the Vedas, Sashtras and puranas. The practices associated with these books shall be declared as punishable.

2. It should be better if the priesthood among Hindus was abolished. Or at least it shall cease to exist as a hereditary right.
3. The priesthood shall be regulated through sanad. The unofficial priesthood shall be banned.
4. The state shall take care of the priesthood appointment
5. The number of priests shall be under control.

This involves the democratization. It should be based on Liberty, Equality and Fraternity, i.e., with democratic principles.[16]

Ambedkar considers that the Upanishadic doctrines shall be brought into the folk lore. Ambedkar feels that Morality and religion, therefore, are not mere matters of likes and dislikes. You may dislike exceedingly a scheme of morality, which, if universally practiced within a nation, would make that nation the strongest nation on the face of the earth. Yet in spite of your dislike such a nation will become strong. You may like exceedingly a scheme of morality and an ideal of justice, which if universally practiced with in a nation, would make it unable to hold its own in the struggle with other nations. Yet in spite of your admiration this nation will eventually disappear. The Hindus must, therefore, examine their religion and their morality in terms of their survival value. This is the first advice given by Dr. B. R. Ambedkar. The second involves the verification and acceptance of their cultural values. The third advice is to check whether they can continue to worship the same old ideals. Fourth the Hindu shall recognize the impermanence of the dogmas and the recognition of the change as the very nature of life.

REFERENCES

1. B.R. Ambedkar, *Social Justice and Political Safeguards for Depressed Classes* (ed.) K.L. Chanchreek, Shree Publishing House, New Delhi, 1991, p. 150.
2. B.R. Ambedkar, *Dr. Babasaheb Ambedkar*, Writtings and Speeches, Vol. 1, Compiled by Vasant Moon, Education Department, Govt. of Maharashtra, Bomabay, 1989, pp. 5-6.
3. *Ibid.*, p. 20.
4. *Ibid.*
5. *Ibid.*

6. *Ibid.*
7. *Ibid.*, p. 21.
8. *Ibid.*, pp. 39-40.
9. *Ibid.*
10. *Ibid.*, p. 22.
11. *Ibid.*, p. 54.
12. *Ibid.*, p. 41.
13. *Ibid.*, p. 57.
14. *Ibid.*, pp. 63-64.
15. *Ibid.*, p. 64.
16. *Ibid.*, p. 76.

5

Gandhi's Views on Non-violence

S.V.G. Choodamani

Mahatma Gandhi is one of most dynamic and effective leaders who world has ever seen or studied. Gandhi was a warrior of truth, a priest of non-violence. He was a model of simplicity and practical idealist. Whatever he touched, he made it more knowledgeable. He had unshakable faith in moral order of the universe. The whole life of Gandhi's thought and action based on truth. He influenced Martin Luther King,Nelson Mandela, Archbishop Desmond Tutu and Aung San Suu Kyi and others who inspires us today.

The greatness of Gandhi isthat he has put a sense of self-confidence in the common man to fight against wrong with just two weapons. –Truth and Non-violence. Gandhi's remarkable life and actions stem from a strong moral character, missionary zeal and undying love and faith in all sections of India's various races and religions. This provided him with the necessary fuel to keep his engine of non-violent revolutionary moving at a quick pace.

Non-violence: The kernel of Gandhi's life message which is eternal and universal and which made him into a mahatma is peace and non-violence. The philosophy of Gandhi is mainly based on twin principles, viz., Truth and Non-violence. According to Gandhi, non-violence is truthfulness. Truth is in separable ingredient of non-violence; they are like the two sides of a coin. A person who follows the principles of truth and non-violence knows no defeat in life.

Etymologically, Ahimsa is composed of three elements a (not) hims (to kill or injured) and a (nominal suffix). So the literal meaning of 'Ahimsa' would be non-killing of living being.

During his search for truth, he made the discovery of non-violence. Truth and non-violence, gradually, became convertible concepts. The values of truth and non-violence were implanted in him, as a result of his upbringing.

To quote Gandhi, "Truth and Non-violence are my two lungs. I cannot live without them. Truth is my religion and Ahimsa is the only way of its realization. My religion based on truth and non-violence. I will not sacrifice truth and non-violence even for the divergence of my country or religion". Truth was God to him, and non-violence was his only means of attaining it. There was no politics without truth for him. Ahimsa to Gandhi is the soul force in human life. If a man avoids violence willingly or knowingly, he is near the concept of perfect Ahimsa, or non-violence, or the absolute truth, or God.

In Gandhian state and society, truth, non-violence and love are the guiding principles. Gandhi's non-violence is based upon truth force or soul force. Gandhi's life is based on truth, non-violence and fearlessness. Gandhi defines non-violence as soul force. Force is of two types, viz., physical and spiritual. We are ordinarily acquainted with physical force. Violence consists of physical force. This is a weapon of brutes. Non- violence distinguishes man from the brute. But man has not yet shed the brute in him.

Gandhi says there is no such thing as defeat in non-violence. Non-violence is a positive force, though negative in expression. It is a force of love. One should love all in order to be non-violent. Gandhi has insisted that no one should be considered an enemy in this world. The message of non-violence is the message of universal love. Gandhi gives a basis for this universal love. The famous saying of Gandhi is "Hate the sin, but not the sinner". When all men are considered to be good, it is easy to practice universal love of non- violence.

Non-violence is positive force. Non-violence means conscious suffering. Satyagraha movements are very good examples of conscious suffering. A non-violent person suffers in the process of exercising of non-violence. He does not like to put others in difficulties and thereby, cause suffering to others. Even if others land him in difficulties, he never thinks of retaliation.

Non-violence is fearlessness. Fear and non-violence cannot go together. A person who is afraid cannot speak truth and hence cannot practice non-violence. Shed fear' is the message of Gandhi. The essence of his non-violence is fearlessness. Non-violence, to be a potent force, must begin with the mind. Non-violence of the mere body, without the co-operation of the mind is non-violence of the weak or the cowardly, and has therefore no potency. Non-violence is possible only for a fair-minded person. Non-violence is the attitude of a developed soul. There should be perfect coordination between the mind and the body for the practice of non-violence. Non-violence is a way of resolving the conflict situation.

Non-violence first of all presupposes the inner purification of the individual. In perfect non-violence, there is no scope for violence, hatred, anger and ill-will for others. Gandhi believes that whenever, wherever there is love there is God. For love, perfect co-ordination of mind, body and speech are required. But such a practice of Ahimsa is the quality of God alone. In the way of non-violence, one's conduct is governed by the dictates of his conscience and convictions. Non-violence implies non-exploitation in every walk of life. viz., social, economic and political. Man is mainly concerned with social, economical conditions in his daily life. Exploitation at any stage is directly affecting the personality of the individual.

Non-violence for him means refraining from inflicting injury on others through malice, anger, harsh-words, exploitation or any type of injustice

Truth without non-violence is not truth. It should be truth in thought and action. Non-violence leads to Sarvodaya type of society. Non-violence is not utilitarianism. Utilitarianism is the theory of the greatest happiness of the greatest number. Non-violence leads from Antyodaya to Sarvodaya. So the final goal of non-violent society is Sarvodaya.

Non- violence is a broad concept. It does not go hand in hand with centralization. Like Truth, non-violence is the compendium of all Gandhian virtues and absolute essentials for humanity.

Non-violent strategy can take up any modern challenge. Non-violence is the relentless pursuit of truthful ends through moral means. For Gandhi, non-violence and truth were one whole. In

Gandhi's mind, truth incarnates as love, and love translates itself into action and incarnates as non-violence.

Ahimsa - the universal principle

According to Gandhi, all religions are agreed to the principle of Ahimsa. A principle is the expression of perfection. As an imperfect being, a man is unable to practice perfection. So far as man lives in flesh and blood, he cannot do without committing some sort of violence

Gandhi wanted Indians to have in them the courage for dying without killing but in case they lacked that courage of self-suffering, he wanted them to cultivate the art of killing and being killed, rather than to flee from danger in a cowardly manner. Gandhi maintained that Ahimsa in its positive form means the largest love, greatest charity. Gandhi's goal was friendship with the whole world and he could combine the greatest love with the greatest opposition to the wrong. Non-violence to Gandhiji was not a resignation from all real fighting against wickedness.

Gandhi was totally against the animal sacrifice. To him, it was violence, as it cannot stand the test of truth and non-violence. He said that he readily admitted his incompetence in vedic scholarship, but he was not worried by this incompetence, so far as animal sacrifice was concerned. According to Gandhi, even if the practice of animal sacrifice be proved a feature of vedic society, it can form no precedent to a votary of ahimsa.

Relevance of Gandhian ideals

Gandhi opined that truth and non-violence are applicable in legislatures, in politics and worldly affairs. He had no use for them to attain individual salvation. All along, it had been his experiment to introduce and apply them in every day life. He strove to make these principles as matters for practice by groups, communities and nations. The non-violent concept of Gandhi should aim at equalizing economic conditions of the people to attain social justice and economic freedom.

Human character is an essential basis for human welfare. Human conduct undergoes different levels of development. These different levels are mainly as follows (1) the level of instinctive conduct (2) the level of customs and manners and (3) the level of conscience or reflection.

Gandhi maintained the welfare of society depends upon man's character, moral qualities and efforts to self improvement. The society changes for the better with the development of human character.

Relevance of Mahatma Gandhi today is asking the question– what is the relevance of the sun to solar system. If he was irrelevant, as many people are bound to say, why is he not forgotten like many other twentieth century thinkers? In the context of growing violence Gandhi philosophy is highly essential.

The crucial problem of the world today is to establish peace. Chronic poverty, pollution, un-employment, exploitation, inequalities and constant threat of war are additional problems. Today humanity is truly at the cross roads. Technology beyond human control is one of the gravest dangers before mankind .Toynbee, "science and technology are man's outstanding success, but human relations are outstanding failure". Everybody is using the youth's energy for a destructive purpose than for constructive purpose.Re-discovering Gandhi becomes global necessity for peace, prosperity, freedom, harmony and survival of the whole human race.

Conclusion

People must translate Gandhiji's ideals into real life. Simplifying our life styles on cutting on consumption as a pre-condition of our peace with poor, of our peace with nature and of our peace with and within ourselves. Happiness can be attained only through adherence to some values. Wealth and standards of living alone do not make for happiness.All of us need to examine ourselves as individuals, to identify, minimize and eliminate double standards and hypocrisy. We re-dedicated ourselves to carry forward his message towards creating a better world.

The works of Dr. Abhay Bang and Dr. Rani Bang with Adivasis, the Narmada Andolan of Medha Patkar, the work of Anna Hazare in village development, many rehabilitation centres for alcoholics and drug addicts, many educational institutions are some of the examples which are working on Gandhian thoughts. The nation should concentrate to pass on Gandhian values to the youth.It is our duty to promote and protect the Gandhian values.

Today, we can also unite under a single belief of non-violence and love in order to eradicate the evils that are holding humankind back from achieving greater peace and justice for all. We need to understand Gandhiji's strategies, learn them and apply them in our everyday lives, wherever appropriate. We may or may not be able to change the entire world. But definitely we can, in our own small way, make a small change to the small world around us.

In the 21st century Gandhian ideals can work better than most other narrow ideologies. Through Gandhian ideology poverty can be eradicated, conflicts could be solved, peace could be achieved and environment could be healed. Let us pledge to follow the ideals of Mahatma. There is no doubt that Gandhi's ideal of Non-violence will be extolled as long as history continues.

REFERENCES

1. M.K., Gandhi, *The Story of My Experiments with Truth*, Navajivan Publishing House, Ahmadabad, 1948.
2. Gandhi, M.K., *Truth*, Navajivan Publishing House, Ahmedabad, 1971.
3. Mahadevan, T.K. (Ed), *Truth and Non-Violence*, Gandhi Peace Foundation, New Delhi, 1969.
4. Prabhu, R.K., (compiled) *Truth is God*, Navajivan Publishing House, Ahmadabad, 1955 & 1969.
5. Ananda Hingorani, (ed.) *God is Truth*, Bharatiya Bhavan.
6. M.K Gandhi, *Young India*, March 10, 1920.
7. *Ibid.*, December 30, 1929.
8. *Ibid., Young India*, April 30, 1925.
9. *Ibid., Young India*, November 4, 1926.
10. *Ibid., Young India*, November 17, 1921.
11. M.K. Gandhi, *The Collected Works of Mahatma Gandhi*, Publication Division, New Delhi, 1958.

SECTION - 2

GANDHIAN IDEOLOGY—RELEVANCE TO CONTEMPORARY SOCIETY

6

Gandhian Ideology: Relevance to Contemporary Society

M.Lakshmipathi Raju

The Teachings of Gandhi – the great and benign lamp of wisdom and humanity are for eternity. He gave us the priceless gift of self-respect and sense of dignity as a nation. His success rested upon the moral grandeur of his soul. He was a fighter who pushed back the mightiest empire on earth without the use of force. He was a spirit of profound wisdom and captivating humility; He was a frail man who confronted the brutality of military strength with the dignity of a simple human being.

Gandhiji said, "We must go back to the spirit and ideas of those halcyon days when we practiced the philosophy of nation first and foremost; when we spoke of the language of the heart, when we breathed the air of idealism, when we walked hand-in-hand on the path of self-less service and sacrifice; when all sons and daughters of the motherland prided themselves in being," Indian first, Indian last and Indian always." The need of the hour is that leaders and people should get inspired by Gandhi's teachings.

Gandhi is believed to have greater relevance in the present world of modern science and technology. Modern science and technology has produced geographical neighbourhood but the distance between man and man has increased. We have become highly individualistic. We feel no longer concerned with each other's welfare, except in commercial and business terms. Cooperation has been replaced by competition and consumerism. Much intelligence and much energy are going in this effort.

Mahatma Gandhi made significant contribution to social development by constructive work and programmes, aiming at removal of disabilities, of the people at the social, political, economic and spiritual levels.

He has given us a new school of thought leading to social development. Gandhiji says that his religion is religion of truth. Instead of saying," God is truth", he has been saying that "truth is god". To be true to Religion, one has to engage himself in continuous service to Humanity.

An indepth study of Gandhian movements will provide a perennial source of inspiration. It should be made an integral part of a programme of social work education. The Gandhian and Professional Social Workers should join together so that the issues relating to injustice are not swept under the carpet.

Gandhiji says: "the human body is meant for service, never for indulgence, renunciation is lfie, indulgence spells death. Service to humanity has been the ideal of all saints and prophets of peace and so for Gandhiji.

Gandhiji's Concept of Renunciation

Gandhiji states that renunciation of the fruits of one's actions is the basic teachings of the 'Gita'. Action is not to be avoided and cannot be avoided. For a man who follows the teachings of the Gita, Sanyas is not actual renunciation of all actions. It is renunciation of the fruits of action as Gandhiji states, and it is also renunciation of the mental attachment to fruits. The Sanyas is state of mind and the true sanyasi makes no difference between human beings. He spends his time for the betterment of all. Gandhiji is clear in saying that.

To uphold Universal norms

As human, we experience the pain of the others only when he or she is part of our moral community. In our increasingly divided polity, that sense of shared moral community across religious and ethnic boundaries is today under severe strain. When there is breakdown of moral order in society, the professional social workers cannot remain just a "conscienceless scientism". It is the duty of the professional social workers as the upholders of universal norms to step in as shown by Gandhi.

The Gandhian thought and principles are not meant for any particular society or region. They are meant for the whole human society. The indications of the age, the world wide inquisitiveness and future needs and aspirations – all point to the necessity that attempt should not be to limit Gandhi within national walls. Gandhi's strategy was that social transformation should began millions 'non-persons' and 'half persons' marginalized Indian Humanity", living on the outskirts of organized society and below the margins of subsistence within the society."

Gandhi believed that " No social order, be it international or national or any lesser unity of human organization, can be considered 'normal' unless the creative energies of these 'Non-persons' and "half persons" are not harnessed fully by making them participate in socio-economic life on the basis of freedom, honour, dignity and equality." Gandhij's constructive programme is a comprehensive instrument of reconstruction which specially included the needs of Non-persons, the outcastes, the half-persons, the castaways and the lowliest and the poorest section of human population.

The thought of Gandhi is the thought of the future. The coming century may be described as a century of Gandhi, and the world today has accepted Gandhi as a model to solve the problems of the present century. Gandhi gave to the world news and revolutionary concepts such as satyagraha (truth force), sarvodaya(welfare of all), and Shanti Sena (peace brigade). In the coming years particularly in the twenty-first century, these Gandhian concepts are found to gain greater relevance. In fact, Gandhi is more relevant to day than ever before. We have to choose between Ahimsa and Atom, Non-violence and Non-existence, and between Sarvodaya and Sarvanasha (total annihilation).

Precept and Practice

Gandhiji always emphasized that "India lives in her villages." He practiced whatever he preached. His thoughts and actions always went together. He used to say that one ounce of action is better than tones of thought without any action. The Professional Social Workers (PSWs) should emulate an example.

Non-violence

The services of violence and unrest show decadence of higher moral and ethical values. The lack of spirit, trust, faith and inter-personal and inter-group involvement and concerns for each other, is suggestive of the fact that the tested path of tolerance, justice, morality and trusteeship shown by the former leaders and specially by Gandhi has been forsaken by present leaders all over the world.

In order to come out of the present malaise and dilemma, the only remedy lies in adopting the Gandhian path to resolve conflicts. Arnold Toynbee has rightly observed. "At this supremely dangerous movement in human history, the only way of salvation for mankind is the Indian Way. Emperor Ashoka's and Mahatma Gandhi's principles of non-violence and Sri Ramakrishna's testimony to the harmony of religions. Here we have an attitude and spirit that can make it possible for the human race to grow together into a single family and in the atomic age; this is the only alternative to destroying ourselves."

To quote Gandhi's own words, "I shall work for an India in which the poorest feel that it is their country in whose making they have effective voice, an India in which there should be no rich class and no poor class of people and an India in which all communities shall live in perfect harmony. This is the India of my dreams. His first dream was fulfilled but the second was not. According to the Mahatma, the true time for celebration would be when the second dream is fulfilled.

Gandhi's Vision about Society

Gandhi envisioned that our hands and acts have got to move towards a society which will really feed, clothe and provide shelter to everybody and treat every body in the world as equal and pave the way to live in peace. We should move towards a society where every one will live in harmony with his neighbour, where everyone will be treated with equal respect, will feel secure, self respect and self-confidence and feels he/she is wanted. Every one realizes that it is only global peace that will make the human race feel safe and happy.

Social Values

It is necessary to transform society through the individual and by social values of love, non-violence and justice. Social workers must create the conditions which would help the people to be self reliant and realize the ideals of the purity, honesty and righteousness, fair play, justice and universal tolerance without the loss of individual freedom. Gandhiji challenged the west – centric model of development. Drawing upon the Gandhian ideas, the Narmada Bachao Andolan (NBA) led by Medha Patkar, a Professional Social Worker has shown the limitations of the state-led development package at the cost of the values of the people, in this case, the displaced tribal's. Service to the people is to be considered on duty, Professional Social Work has to be a way of life, not just a mere profession to earn money, name and fame.

A. Basic Values of Development

The modern development activities have tended to create avenues for excessive consumerism of some against the continued deprivation of many others. Gandhiji had clearly advocated the restrictions of wants voluntarily. In fact he had said that there is enough in this world to meet the needs of everybody, but not enough to meet even a single man's greed. Development may be defined as economic growth plus social change, as bread plus dignity, as a technical solution to underdevelopment, as institutional building, human development, a more equitable distribution of resources. The basic values of development are human dignity, equality and social justice. Another principle implied in social development is the emphasis on cooperation as against competition. It lays emphasis on collectivity as against rugged individualism.

By development Gandhi meant not economic development but social development, that is, development of weaker sections, particularly scheduled castes and scheduled tribes. Gandhiji was against industrialization and large scale production; he is in favour of small scale industries and cottage industries. Gandhiji said, mass productions create mass unemployment. He was also against concentration of wealth in a few individuals and wide disparities of incomes between rich and the poor. In social work practice, we emphasize growth with justice and equitable distribution. Hence Gandhian values and social work go together.

A.P.J.Abdul Kalam, while addressing the three-day international conference on the occasion of Golden Jubilee of Indian Parliament on 23-1-2003 said, " that poverty, illiteracy and unemployment were sowing seeds of terrorism world wide. He exhorted the delegates that global sharing of resources to address these issues for world peace and development is essential. In other words, when there is "a will" in the leaders, there is a way and the way as shown by Gandhiji." In everything that he did therefore the "common man" was before his eyes. The common man has lost his self-respect and his soul. It is most unfortunate that Gandhiji's ideas and words not commanded attention from professional social workers that is justly due.

The Gandhian model envisaged that development and governance should be bottom-up and not be top-down; goal should be self defined and not stranger –defined ; production should be aimed at basic goods to fulfil basic values with useful value and not at non-basic and greed-oriented luxury goods; the process of production should be by the masses and not through mass production and the whole approach should be holistic and not sectoral. The Gandhian model in the words of J.C.Kumarappa, leads to decentralized economic planning and actually 'Economics of permanence, while in the model of industrial economy there is the danger that the rich becomes the richer. The need of the hour is that leaders and people of the country be inspired by the ideals and teachings of Mahatma Gandhi.

The Gandhian model of development: requires active involvement and participation of man building his own destiny. This is possible if some of us belong to so called rich and middle class voluntarily instead of drifting towards consumerism are willing to sacrifice and share our pleasures in the interest of down-trodden of our society.

Gandhi as Communicator

Gandhi was a great communicator. Realizing the impact of communication on the people that Gandhi had wielded, Sir J.H. Holmes wrote, in 1920s: "This man holds absolutely in his hands today the destinies of his people. When Gandhi speaks, India speaks. When Gandhi acts, it is India that acts. When Gandhi is arrested, it is the India that is outraged and humiliated. More truly, I believe than any other man who has ever lived, this great Indian is the incarnation of a peoples soul." He further commented: "He holds today the centre of world's is attention. This position of primary is now occupied by a little oriented who has never held any official position who seeks neither glory nor power." The best quality of the communicator must possess is to practice what he preaches.

Constructive Programmes

Gandhi carried constructive programmes and did not call them social work programmes. He carried them alongside the freedom movement. His constructive programmes included, abolition of untouchability, promoting community amity through the removal of all distinctions, introduction of prohibition, development of rural industries, introduction of basic education, emancipation of women, organization of peasantry, improvement of village sanitation, upliftment of Advasis, and improvement of the cattle. The social workers would find these programmes enriching Indian society in general and rural society in particular.

Gandhiji's strong adherence to high social ideals as practical approach inspired sincere and conscientious workers to follow him with a genuine sense of dedication. His belief in the potential of rural India, and the wisdom that India lives in villages guided him to concentrate his efforts on villages. Rural reconstruction was his mission. He initiated a large number of constructive social welfare programmes designed to remove the evils that had crept into society. His constructive programme found ready acceptance among people. The success of his power weapon satyagraha too enticed many volunteers.

Vinoba Bhave who came forward with the novel idea of Bhoodan and Gramdan Movment (land and village gift) and Jayaprakash Narayan along with others inculcated the Gandhian spirit of voluntarism. A.V.Thakkar, popularly known as Thakkar Bapa, who made a mark in the history of voluntary service, too based his work on gandhian principles. His attention was drawn to the field of education, health and tribal development.

Gandhi and Environment

The concept of environmental conservation and survival of human beings was inherent in the ideology of Mahatma Gandhi.

Gandhi was ahead of his time and a precursor of environmentalism. As early as 1927, he warned the world that large scale industrialism would create problems of the type we are confronted with today.

Nature is becoming the victim of human greed. Indiscriminate misuse of natural resources in the name of economic development and disregard of the ecological implications, has brought mankind to the present impasse. Gandhi stated that " the earth provides enough to satisfy every man's need but not every man's greed." He was of the view that as long as greed prevailed and the fruits of economic development were not shared equitably among the masses, poverty and hunger would exist. The present ecological crisis demand a different worldview. Giving up the present life style and a reduction in consumerism would directly support the gandhian ideology of simple living and high thinking.

Man must realize that he does not own nature. His is only one of its many offsprings. Nature is not due to man, man is due to nature. He is among its components. More importantly, the wisest animal on earth should play the role of "trustee" of nature's enormous wealth. Exploiting nature ruthlessly amounts to genocide and hence is a crime. Every living component of nature has a right to a dignified existence. Being the most evolved, man should be the "custodian" and protector of the dignity of all. (M.K.Gandhi)

The important elements of gandhian environmentalism can be summed up as follows: (1) human beings should act as though they are part of nature rather than apart from nature. (2) Materials available on earth should not be used with an element of greed, (3) human beings should practice non-violence not only towards fellow humans but also towards other living organisms and inanimate materials because overuse of such materials also amounts to violence. (4) a conservationist and sustainable life-saving approach should prevail over a consumerist self destructive approach ; (5) humans rarely think about how much is enough for a simple, need-based, austere and comfortable life-style; (6) ethics and self-discipline in resource use is an overriding criterion of development.

Bhoodan and Gramdan

Gandhi's idea of sarvodaya (the welfare of all) envisaged a reconstructed Indian village society with people using simple hand-tools in agriculture and industry, engaged in production for local use rather than profit. It was a society of equals, a kind of communitarians, wherein each individual would place the common welfare above their own selfish interests and the principle of "from each according to their ability, to each according to their need" would be paramount. The vision of a society of small, largely self-sufficient village communities, a just and non-violent political, social and economic order, was fare removed from the modern industrial society that Nehru eagerly anticipated.

To Vinoba, the movement is either the first step towards a total revolution of society, a revolution through love. The movement was calling not for the individuals surrender of a proportion of their land and but for the complete surrender of property rights in favour of the village community. Under the revised gramdan scheme, the privatee use of land was to continue, whilst the formal ownership of the land was vested in the village community. Vinoba's goal was to usher in a three-fold revolution. "Firstly, I want to change the people's heart. Secondly, I want to create a change in their lives. Thirdly, I want to change the social structure ... we do not aim at doing mere acts of kindness, but creating a kingdom of kindness.

Sarvodaya and Social Work

Sarvodaya aims at a complete transformation of the present social structure through quite , constructive, social work carried on primarily at the village level and in slum area, with a view to initiating a non-violent revolution and establishing a more just social order. Sarvodaya draws its inspiration as much from the ancient religious traditions as from the modern, national secular, humanitariasm or revolutionary idealism. It looks upon service to society as the raison d'etre of main's life on earth. In this sense, sarvodaya is all social work and nothing else. The ideology of sarvodaya is not a product of intellectual theorization. It grew out of activities, experiences and inner conviction of great soul, i.e Gandhi who wanted to do away with all kinds of social disabilities, injustices and inequalities.

Gandhian Ideology: Relevance to social work practice

While Gandhiji had struggled for awakening, enlightenment, freedom and socio-economic justice for one and all, his utmost priority had been to serve the weakest of the weak. He tirelessly worked to strengthen the "weakest link", the poorest of the poor. This basic principle of human and social policy should be the aim of Professional Social Workers. The country cannot have a better ideal than that provided by Gandhiji to work with workers as well as Professional Social Workers.

To revamp Social Work

To revamp and change the content of social work education to suit to the contemporary needs of the society the following areas need emphasis in social work education.

1) Peace movements and peace studies
2) Resolution of conflicts
3) Policies, programmes and strategies for development of scheduled castes and scheduled tribes and other backward classes.
4) Anti-poverty programmes and their impact on poor and welfare programmees.
5) Sarvodaya (Gandhian Model) Vs Western model of development.
6) Panchayat Raj System to build participating democracy from grassroots upwards.; and

Social Worker's intervention or touch must make a 'common man' a capable and an effective citizen fully participating and decision –making in governance of his own affairs. Most of the Indian teachers diminish Gandhi as totally irrelevant to the practice of social work. Gandhi was a great social activist but our social work educators and practitioners do not find any maternal relevance in Gandhian literature that would enrich the methods of the profession. On the contrary, American professor alinsky, has elaborately quoted Gandhi to draw sanction for his theory of social action and methods.(Gandhi, 2002).

To Work with the Poor and Oppressed

In the light of Gandhian ideology, the role of Professional

Social Workers(PSW) involves various tasks, first, worker should positively discriminate to work amongst those who have benefited least, or not at all the from government programmes. That is, worker should work with the poor and oppressed who has least access to aid and resources. Secondly it is important that the worker works with groups as opposed to individuals because it is only as groups that people can have the bargaining power necessary to achieve their goals. Thirdly, the task of the worker is to initiate the process of conscientization – of critical awareness by getting people to formulate and articulate their desires about issues important to them. It is most important that these are their issues and not those preconceived by the worker. The worker should encourage people to analyze their situation, thus activating some of their critical abilities.

To protect Human Rights and environment

Prof. S.N. Renede suggests that "Social Workers and educators have a special role and stake in helping to build up peace movement. Such movement cannot succeed unless policy makers and made to realize that real succeed unless policy maker are made to realize that real defence and security lie in ensuring the well being of the people, and not suppressing their discontent." Welfarism must be seen in terms of human rights. Both environment and human rights must envelop all mankind, and social work must become part of the movement for the protection of both." The deteriorating ecological environment, illiteracy, lack of access to opportunity, social conflict and dire poverty of the disadvantaged groups need to be addressed.

To act as communicators

Social workers have to move forward to meet the challenges of the difficult decades that lied ahead. They have to be enlightened and perceptive communicators, articulate with minds of their own. They should be able to cope with the demands of increasingly complicated policies and programmes of development. They should be able to interact with the politicians, administrators, scientists and eminent persons in their walks of life as well as with common people.

The progress of social change would be faster and smoother and development goals can be realized more speedily and effectively if the social workers are able to involve poor people to participate in policy formulation and implementation of programmes meant for their through appropriate modalities of communication.

To strengthen and develop dalits

Salvation of Social Work Profession lies in moving towards rural and tribal areas and giving dalits a top priority in their work. This is because the man belonging to the Fourth state(or poor) or the common man of India or for that matter of the third world of today as well as of tomorrow and after belong to rural and tribal India. To restore vitality to the Indian society and build up the future prosperity of the common man, it is necessary to strengthen and develop Dalits. Only then, and in that process, the well being of the Indian people will be realized.

Social Work is both pathiative as well as responsible for changing institutions. It helps individuals in the frame work of existing conditions as well as to help change social institutions. It recognizes the multiple causation of problems and realizes that the cause lie neither exclusively in the individual nor in the societal structure. It becomes clear that profession which works towards social justice in a wide sense must feel responsible for amelioration and social change. The change should begin from within to influence the policies at various levels to change the flight of Dalits.

REFERENCES

1. Chowdary, G.P., (ed) , (1985). *Relevance of Gandhism,* Capital Publishing House, Delhi.
2. Gangrade, K.D , *Gandhian Approach to Development and Social Work,* Concept Publishing Company, New Delhi, (2005),
3. Sharma, S.V. (1982). *Gandhi Vignan,* Vol 6, No.I, October 1982, Journal of Academy of Gandhian Studies.
4. Singh, R.R (ed.) (1995). *Association of Schools of Social Work in India,* Delhi School of Social Work, Delhi.

7

Gandhiji's Contribution to Indian Society: Social Work Perspective

Saraswati Raju Iyer

Mahatma Gandhi has rightly been called the "Father of the Nation." It was under his leadership that India won her independence. He followed various methods to achieve his objectives. He started the Non-cooperation movement, the civil disobedience movement. He defied the might of the British Empire. However, by doing all these he made the nationalist movement a mass movement and thereby brought about the independence of the country.

Background of Mahatma Gandhi

The original name of Mahatma Gandhi was Mohandas Karamchand Gandhi. He was born on 2nd October 1869 at Porbander in Kathiawad and was shot dead at New Delhi on 30th January 1948 (at 79 years). His father was a Dewan of a petty state in Gujarat. He went to England for qualifying himself for the Bar. On return he practiced law in Bombay. Gandhiji went to South Africa in connection with professional work on behaf of a Mohammedan firm. His stay in South Africa was the formative period of his life. It was in South Africa that he put into practice his weapon of Satyagraha. He also developed self – confidence among his countrymen to face a struggle. It was in that Dark Continent that he taught his countrymen to give up fear, resist evil by truth and never to yield and strive to rise to the full stature of manhood.

The Transmission from Reform to Welfare

The emergence of Mahatma Gandhi in 1920 as a political leader and Social reformer in Indian public life has to be viewed in the historical context. Several social and political reformers and thinkers had appeared on the Indian scene during the eighteen and nineteenth centuries but none of them had succeeded in arousing the emotions of the masses as Gandhiji did. Gandhiji's influence was incomparable inspired by him, the political movement, infused with the spirit of social reform became a National Movement participated in by all, irrespective of caste, creed or community. In other words the all important steps were taken from reform to welfare. An ascetic and a politician he combines in himself all the modern Indian Reform Movements – he fights untouchability, drunkenness and pauperism. He started a Trade Union Movement and a National University; as devout Vaishnavite he yet gives a new depth and meaning to Ahimsa, and Satya, He practiced what he preached. He taught himself the virtue of self-discipline before he conveyed. The greatest political leader of India founds an order of Sanyasis and creates an army of volunteers.

As a social worker or reformer Gandhi instilled in each man an awareness of his social and economic responsibilities. He inculcated the feeling of respect for self as well as for others. His emphasis was on duties rather than rights. The secret of his influence on people lay in its appeal to the heart rather than to the mind.

We call Gandhi a charismatic leader because he was not always a religious leader alone but as well as a political and social leader. A charismatic leader is always a radical who challenges established practice by going to the root of the matter. He dominates men by virtue of qualities inaccessible to others and incompatible with the rules of thought and action that govern everyday life.

Gandhiji was not born a missionary. He acquired that zeal for service during his two decades in South Africa – where he was deeply engrossed in the cause of establishing rights of citizenship for the members of his "Coolie nation". With his own self disciplined ways he conveyed to the masses of self purification and appealed for disciplined organized action to overcome all social, economic and political ills. He always expressed concern for the well-being of others – especially for the underprivileged, the wronged and the oppressed. He disciplined the demoralized people of India and made them work – not by force or any material inducement but by a gentle look, and a soft word above all his personal example.

Gandhiji's Interest in Social Service

Service to the poor was his heart desire and it has always thrown him among the poor people with whom he identified himself. This ability to identify himself with the people Gandhi considered an indispensable asset for entry into any form of relationship with fellow human being. The reason for his entire absorption in service to the community was the desire for self realization. He said that he had made the religion of service his own as he felt that God could be realized only through service. This total dedication through service is a quality not always found among leaders and workers who are engaged in social service and social welfare work. Gandhiji's unique quality was that he rendered service and performed humanitarian work in a joyful spirit. He was greatly influenced by Ruskin's book "*Unto the Last*" which he translated into Gujarati under the title "Sarvodaya" (Welfare of all). He summed up its teachings as follows:

1. That the good of the individual is contained in the good of all.
2. Equality of services – that the work of a barber had as much as value of a lawyer's work – as all have the same right of earning their livelihood.
3. That a life of labourer i.e., the life of the tiller of the soil and the handicrafts men is the life worth living.

Gandhiji wrote that he will strive for the greatest good of all and die with the same attempt to realize the ideal. He will therefore be willing to die so that others may have life. Gandhiji aimed at achieving the good of the individual as an integral part of the good of all people. For the first time he instilled among his people a sense of the dignity of labour and inculcated a feeling of pride in all kinds of work. Whether in South Africa or India he moved among untouchables and lepers with perfect ease. This exhibited the sense of his sincerity.

Gandhiji's goal was not just the achievement of political freedom but elimination of feuds and discords among the religious and caste groups. Therefore he concentrated on the problems of disciplining the masses to self-reliance of raising women to a plane of political, economic and social equality with men re-examining the religious habits which divided the nation and cleansing Hinduism of its social abomination of untouchability. Patriotism to Gandhiji meant the welfare of the people and the welfare of the people depended upon an acceptance of the dignity of labour.

Sarvodaya (the welfare of all) eventually became the word that represented Gandhiji's ideas of welfare. In order to reach this goal he adopted a programme of dual purpose:

1. Changing the Indians for the better and
2. Forcing the British to get out of India.

He recognized the interdependence of both these actions and stressed the importance of carrying them out simultaneously. He advocated that "everyone should have enough for his needs. Everyone must have balanced diet, a decent house to live in, facilities for education of one's children and adequate medical relief". So he worked for the greatest good of all considering this the end and purpose of all individual activity as well as of all social activity. His welfare and social reform activities were an integral part of his life. It is man's dependence on society that teaches him the lesson of humanity. Gandhiji visualized democracy as a form of government under which the weakest should have same opportunity as the strongest. The true source of right becomes duty in a democratic situation. He valued individual freedom but he said the man should not forget that he is essentially a social being.

With the appearance of Gandhiji on the Indian scene, social welfare began to change from its conceptual form into a more organized system of social services and institutions designed to aid individuals and groups to attain satisfying standard of life and health. The many Ashrams established by Gandhiji may be viewed both as centres for training social welfare workers and as settlement, house... resembling particularly the universal settlement houses with the modification to suit Indian conditions. The Ashrams founded by Gandhiji conveyed both the goal and method of service. They lived a common life-shared together thus bringing together different caste groups to break bread inspite of caste barriers.

Sarvodaya and Social Work

The concept of Sarvodaya is much older in origin. The concept of professional social work is about a century old. Sarvodaya is broader concept than social work. Its goal is welfare of all and creation of stateless and classless society through Boodan, Gramdan, Gramswaraj, Santhi Sena and non-violence. Social work aims at helping individuals within their own selves or in their own environment to solve their problems. Sarvodaya emphasizes truth and non-violence and the basic goodness of the man, social work while upholding the values of dignity of man emphasizes also acceptance of individual's right to self determination and confidentiality. The values of social work are not based in particular individual's philosophies of life and action; they have developed on the basis of experience of practitioners over a period of time. The ideology of Sarvodaya is not a product of intellectual theorization; it grew out of activities, experience and inner conviction of a great soul to remove social disabilities, injustices and inequalities. Social work has drawn its knowledge from psychology, sociology and other social sciences, developed into a science of its own.

Gandhiji's Basic Philosophy

Gandhiji emphasized respect for human dignity and envisaged the freedom of the nation as the first condition for due respect to the dignity of its inhabitants. Gandhiji's acceptance of people regardless of differences of religion, caste or national background, was reflected in all work, in his speeches and public utterances. It was the people who mattered to him and not their background in terms of social, religious, economic or political affiliation. Time and again he insisted that one should not impose one's own ideas or views on other people; believed that people would change only by their own conviction not through super imposition of another's views. Gandhiji believed that self-help is the best help that people function better when they are involved in the process of making plans, programmes etc. Gandhiji preached and practiced self – discipline as a way of life. According to him truth and non-violence are matters for the practice not only for the individual but also for the groups, community and nation. He based his philosophy based on the two ruling principles of his life truth (Satya) and non – violence (Ahimsa) to the solution of individual and social problems. He also envisaged the purity of means, Satyagraha as the universal principle of life that works in all human relations. The twentieth century had been considered by some as the age of Mahatma Gandhi. He successfully combined the political movement for freedom with social reform and social welfare. Gandhiji's value system has moulded the social policy of the Government of India since the achievement of Independence.

Mahatma Gandhi and Satyagraha

Satyagraha according to Mahatma Gandhi is literally holding on to the truth and it means truth force. Truth is soul or spirit. It is therefore known as soul-force. It is not a passive spirituality or passive resistance but extremely active force; suffering, According to Gandhiji, it purifies the sufferers, intensifies favourable public opinion and it makes a direct appeal to the soul of the oppressor.

The Satyagrahi seeks to convert his opponent by his noble character and suffering. The Satyagrahi is never prepared to yield any position which he holds to be the truth. The purer he is and the more he suffers, the quicker the progress. In Satyagraha there is no place for hatred or ill will.

The technique of Satyagraha may take the following forms – 1. Non-cooperation, 2. Civil-Disobedience, 3. Hijrat, 4. Fasting and 5. Strike. The issue for which Satyagraha is launched should be true and substantial. The Satyagrahi should make himself ready to undergo all kinds of humiliation and suffering. He must prepare himself even to sacrifice his life if occasion demands.

The etymological meaning of the word Sarvodaya is 'Sarva'- 'Udaya' 'Uplift of all'. However it has been translated also as 'Good of all', Service to all and welfare of all', "Gandhian Socialism" and "Co operative common wealth" Mahatma Gandhi coined this term in 1904 in his attempt to paraphrase John Ruskin's 'Unto the last". Antyodaya means the rise or welfare of the poorest of the poor in the society or the rise of the individuals in the lowest strata of the society.

Bhoodan has been made the main plank of Sarvodaya movement by Vinoba because land is the most universal and intimate property of the individual in India. He has combined the

Bhoodan movement with the health labour and Brain gift movement. The objective of Bhoodan movement is that everybody must make his contribution to the good of society as a whole.

Satyagraha

Events were so shaping themselves in Johannesburg as to make this self-purification on the part of Mahatma Gandhi a preliminary as it were to Satyagraha. It can be seen that all the principal events of Gandhi's life, culminating in the vow of brahmacharya, were secretly preparing him for it. The principle called Satyagraha came into being before that name was invented. Indeed when it was born, Gandhi himself could not say what it was. In Gujarati also we used the English phrase 'passive resistance' to describe it. When in a meeting of Europeans Gandhi found that the term 'passive resistance' was too narrowly construed, that it was supposed to be a weapon of the weak, that it could be characterized by hatred, and that it could finally manifest itself as violence, he had to demur to all these statements and explain the real nature of the Indian movement. It was clear that a new word must be coined by the Indians to designate their struggle.

But Gandhi could not find out a new name, and therefore offered a nominal prize through Indian Opinion to the reader who made the best suggestion on the subject. As a result Maganlal Gandhi coined the word Satyagraha (Sat: truth, Agraha: firmness) and won the prize. But in order to make it clearer Gandhi changed the word to Satyagraha which has since become current in Gujarati as a designation for the struggle.

The history of this struggle is for all practical purposes a history of the remained Gandhi's life in South Africa and especially of his experiments with truth in that sub-continent. He wrote the major portion of this history in Yeravda jail and finished it after he was released. It was published in Navajivan and subsequently issued in book form. Sjt. Valji Govindji Desai has been translating it into English for Current Thought.

To conclude one could understand 'Satyagraha' as Truth (satya) which implies love, and firmness (agraha) bringing about and therefore serving as a synonym for force. Thus Gandhi began to call the Indian movement 'Satyagraha', that is to say, the force which is born of Truth and Love or non-violence, and gave up the use of the phrase 'passive resistance', in connection with it.

Gandhiji's View on Satyagraha

The idea of Satyagraha is the main principle of Gandhism. It is the pivotal point on which his other theories are based. Satyagraha literally means truth force. It is a resistance of all that is evil, impure and untrue through the force of truth and love. Satyagraha has some techniques. They are:

1. Non-Cooperation
2. Civil Disobedience
3. Hijarat
4. Fasting and
5. Strike.

Non-Cooperation may be started by three methods:

1. Hartal
2. Social ostracism
3. Picketing.

Gandhi suggested Satyagraha as means and method for fighting against a powerful enemy.

Principles of Satyagraha

The idea of Satyagraha is the main principle of Gandhism. It is the pivotal point on which his other theories are based. Satyagraha literally means truth force. It is a resistance of all that is evil, impure, untrue and violent through the force of truth and love. About Satyagraha Gandhiji wrote, "Non-violent resistance to political authority, non cooperation with evil and fasting constitute essential parts of it but they do not exhaust its full import". It is the application of moral weapons like truth and love to resist physical force.

Difference between Satyagraha and Passive Resistance

Satyagraha is different from passive resistance. No doubt, both are methods of meeting aggression, settling conflicts and bringing about social and political changes. However, the two differ from each other fundamentally.

1. Passive resistance is a political weapon of expediency but Satyagraha is a moral weapon based on the superiority of soul force over physical force.

2. Passive resistance is the weapon of the weak but Satyagraha is the weapon of the brave who have the courage of dying without killing.
3. A passive resister aims at embarrassing opponent into submission. A Satyagrahi aims at weaning the opponent from error by love and patient suffering.
4. There is hardly any place for love for the opponent in the case of passive resistance. In Satyagrahi, there is no room for hatred or ill will.

It is thus clear that Satyagraha is the struggle with violent force by the spiritual force of the soul; by love and "ahimsa".

Technique of Satyagraha

Satyagraha has some techniques. They are:

1. Non-Cooperation,
2. Civil Disobedience,
3. Hijarat,
4. Fasting, and
5. Strike.

1. Non-cooperation

This is to be directed against a government or authority. It may be started by three methods namely 1. Hartal, 2. Social ostracism and 3. Picketing.

2. Civil Disobedience

It is the non-obedience to law; it is "a complete effective and bloodless substitute of armed revolt." Disobedience should always be civil and never criminal; it should assume the form of non-violent revolt.

3. Hijrat

It means voluntary exile to escape from oppression and injustice. When it becomes impossible for the satyagrahi to live in his home country with honour and self-respect Gandhiji advised him to leave the country as a remedy.

4. Fasting

It is a means of self-purification. It is a dangerous weapon or resistance. It requires both physical and mental courage on the part of the satyagrahi to make it effective.

5. Strike

It is a weapon of the labourers to remedy their legal demand against the owners. Gandhiji's view of strike however, is different from that advocated by the socialists and the communists. According to him, strike is a voluntary, purificatory suffering undertaken to covert the erring opponent. It should be non-violent and disciplined in application.

Is Sayagraha Practicable?

It was considered by many that the methods of struggle, as preached by Gandhiji could not be put into practice and provided no practical solutions against oppression. But as the time passed, these methods established their effectiveness and we find that through them Gandhiji was in a position to relieve Indians from miseries in South Africa and also could win freedom for India from the world's mightiest empire. These methods, however, require proper disciplining and training of mind. If one has these qualities, there is no reason to doubt the practicability of these methods for fighting against any oppression. Therefore, to doubt the effectiveness of these methods is not justified at all.

Conclusion

Gandhi propounded Sarvodaya which denotes way of life or ideology based on truth and non violence. Its goal is to create a stateless and classless society through non-violent means. Sarvodaya included 18 items of work such as khadi and village industries, communal harmony, abolition of untouchability, village sanitation, basic education, prohibition etc. It aimed at making village communities self-reliant. After the death of Gandhiji Vinoba Bhave started Bhoodan Movement. Bhoodan involves donations from individuals and Gramdan involves community action. In Bhoodan the beneficiaries are individuals or group of individuals; under Gramdan beneficiaries are the whole community. The programme unites haves and have – nots and generates a feeling of sharing. Inspite of the efforts of large number of workers Gramdhan movement has not been able to achieve its desired results. In short Gandhiji's Sarvodaya movement, the concepts of

Satyagraha and non-violence have made a tremendous contribution to the Indian society.

REFERENCES

1. *Encyclopaedia of Social Work in India,* Volume three, Publications Division, Ministry of Welfare, Government of India, Delhi Press, New Delhi. 1987.

2. Friedlander, A.W. *Introduction to Social Welfare,* Prentice Hall, Inc, New York, 1955.

3. Gandhi, M.K. *An Autobiography or the Story of My Experiments with Truth,* Navajivan Trust, Ahmedabad. 1927.

4. Gandhi, M.K. *The Story of My Life,* Navajivan Publishing House, Ahmedabad, 2008.

5. Misra, P.D. *Social Work - Philosophy and Methods,* Inter-India Publications, New Delhi, 1994.

6. Moorthy.M.V. *Social Work Philosophy Methods and Fields,* Library of Social Work & Social Work Education, Karnatak University, Dharwar, Karnataka University Press, 1974.

7. Paul Chowdhry. D. *Introduction to Social Work- History,* Concept, Methods and Fields, Atma Ram & Sons, Delhi, 1964.

8

Gandhi and Social Action: The Educational Perspective

V. Krishnamurthy & R.V.L.N. Ratnakara Rao

Gandhi consecrated his whole life and work to the serve of his people. Gandhi is the sage of the scientific age. He repeatedly warned against the indiscriminate use of science and technology in the name of progress. He warnings have come true in the degradation of an environment becoming a strong enemy of mankind. Gandhi advocated a new system of education appropriate to the Indian socio-economic conditions. This Basic education or Nai Talim (New Education) stands as the unique contribution of Gandhi which also involves socio-economic activities like involvement of students in learning a craft, developing kitchen garden to improve self-sufficiency of the school. Similarly, making the mother-tongue as the medium of instruction keeps the school atmosphere home-like and at the same time facilitates the students to understand the concepts taught in the classroom, thus psychologically an appropriate media. Gandhi defined education as the all-round drawing out of the best in child and man-body, mind and spirit. This broader view of education made basic education holistic in the sense that it is not merely literacy but capacity-building and personality development as well as intellectual development and character development as an essential criterion in the progress of the society as a whole. To achieve this, he wants us to include art education, physical education, health education, recreation , moral education and value education in the curriculum so that the child acquires an all-round development of the body, mind and spirit and achieved self-

sufficiency and stability. He says what better book can there be than the book of humanity. He made humanity as the focus in his scheme of educational plan. However, we have not taken his words seriously and did not give a fair-chance for basic education but rather opted the western , English medium corporate schools in the name of liberalisation, privatisation and globalization. As a result , the objective of universal free and compulsory education still remains a dream and is not in the reach of over one-third of school going population as the average literacy rate is around 65% only, thus making the so called largest democracy as a backward, poor illiterate democracy, pushing the country to the level of a satellite nation and not an independent nation in the gamut of the world nations. This paper examines the educational perspective of Gandhi.

The foundation that Macaulay laid (1835)

This refers to Macaulay's 'Minute in Education' in 1835. It laid down the policy of providing public funds for education in the English language and of withdrawing of public support for education in Arabic and Sanskrit. It was not Macaulay's intention to make English the lingua franca of the Indian masses but only of the Indian elites.

> 'To give millions a knowledge a English is to enslave them. The foundations that Macaulay's laid of education has enslaved us'... ' I do not suggest that he had any intention but that has been the result.'

During his 1909 stage in London, Gandhi became acquainted with Lloyd George's language policy and due from it certain conclusions for India:

> 'India will be aroused when we touch all the Indian languages with the spirit of patriotism. Mr. Lloyd George was born in Wales, a principality in Great Britain. It has a dialect of its own and Mr. Lloyd George is taking steps to ensure that Welsh children do not forget their language. How much more need is there for Indians to preserve their languages than for the Welsh to preserve theirs, and how much more keen should we be ?' (CW.9:492)

Gandhi makes a noteworthy distinction between using English for the acquisition of secular Knowledge and using the mother tongue for the acquisition of ethical Knowledge.

Establishment of the Phoenix Settlement for the formation of the New Gandhian personality

The reading of 'Unto The Last' produced two immediate results. The first was the Gandhi's 'decision to establish the Phoenix Settlement, a community of friends who shared in his new discovered convictions. It remained the proto type of the three other communities or Ashrams, he founded later in his life, the Tolstoy Farm outside Johannesburg, the Sabaramati Ashram outside Ahemdabad, and Sevagram outside Wardha.

And the second was to serialize a nine part paraphrase of Ruskin's book in *'Indian Opinion'* and later to publish it as a pamphlet under the title Sarvodaya, a name which he also gave to his newly formulated economic philosophy. The title *Unto The Last* came from St. Matthew, 20:14. Gandhi gave it the title Sarvodaya for the sake of'Indians who do not know English'. Other adaptations also followed. Ruskin has postulated 'social affection' as the basic principle of a humane economy, in place of 'self interest', and 'competition' postulated by modern political economy. Gandhi understood 'social affection' in terms of the Hindu concept of daya or compassion. Ruskin wanted to moderate the forces of the market by the principle of honour. If the clergy man are soldier could work for honour, not profit, why not the business man or industrialist?. And Gandhi understood honour in terms not of obligation of status but of equality and satya (truth). Finally Ruskin saw the value of handicrafts even in an industrial society: Gandhi saw the value of this spinning wheel and the handicrafts for the whole of India.

Prior to writing *Hind Swaraj*, Gandhi experimented with educational reforms by establishing the Phoenix school at Phoenix Settlement. (the Phoenix Settlement which he established in 1904, just outside Durban and where *Hind Swaraj* was first printed.). It was here he conducted his first experiments in developing their sense of All India consciousness free from the harmful effects of modern civilization, undue regionalism, and the worst manifestation of that caste mentality. It was here too that Indian women were able to find liberation from a number of social taboos to which their counter parts in India were still subject. "Phoenix is intended to be a nursery for producing the right men (and women) and right Indians, "he wrote. 'Whatever the energy is put forth in Phoenix is not so much taken away from India, but it is so much given to India... Phoenix is a more suitable place for making experiments and gaining proper training. Where as India, there may be undesirable restraints, there are no such undesirable restraints in Phoenix. For instance, Indian ladies would never come out so boldly as they are doing at Phoenix. The rest of the social customs would have been too much for them'. (CW 9: 382). The Phoenix school planned to incorporate certain features of the ancient system. 'Those in Phoenix who lived with their families can taken up to eight boarders. It is intended that the boys who may be accepted as boarders will be treated as one's own children. This practice prevailed in India in olden days, and it should be revived as far as possible.' (CW 9: 135).

Ruskin's Unto This Last (1860)

It was the second book of Ruskin's *Unto The Last* (1860) that had the more profound impact on Gandhi. The Autobiography speaks of 'the magic spell of this book which he read in 1904 on a night journey from Johannesburg to Durban. It produce an almost instantaneous change in him. The following is the account of what he learned from that book:

1. That the good of the individual is contained in the good of all.
2. That a lawyer's work has the same value as the barber's, in as much as all have the same right of earning their livelihood from their work.
3. That a life of labour, i.e., the life of the tiller of the soil and the handicrafts man, is the life work living.

The first of these I knew. The second I had dimly realized. The third had never occurred to me.... I rose with the dawn, ready to reduce these principles into practice.' (CW 39 : 239)

Tolstoy Farm outside Johannesburg (1910)

Tolstoy Farm was established outside Johannesburg on land donated by his friend Hermann Kallenbach. A second attempt was made on Tolstoy Farm between 1911 and 1913. About 25 boys and girls from different castes and religions were enrolled. The curriculum included arithmetic, Indian history and geography, religious instructions, manual work and sandal making (CW 11:251-2;39:266-73)

Gandhi: The "practical idealist"

No one realized better than Gandhi the tragedy of speculative thought without social action and of social action without true reflection. Living in India, he had understood the aridity and futility of thought divorced from social action, of theory divorced from practice, of intellectual speculation divorced from pragmatic truth and from reflection anchored to concrete situations and problems. What should, therefore, attract a social to Gandhi is his insistence on the primacy of rational thought as the basis of social action. The social philosophy that sustained his life-work and life-style was as eclectic and "open-ended" as Gandhi himself. To my mind, this is why Gandhi is so relevant to the modern world. Marx was a system-builder. According to many today, Marx stood for an "open-ended" system of thought. He was scared of Marxists who tried to convert it into a closed system. Gandhi was no system-builder, and yet he stood for a system of social thought which was "open-ended" system. It had a clarity of design which we have to recapture in the present generation for our own enlightenment. An "open-ended" system of social philosophy has one essential characteristic—unity of thought and practice. The primacy of this unity was recognized by both Gandhi and Marx, but Gandhi understood it as part of his philosophy of social action in his own characteristic fashion. He called himself a "practical idealist" in the sense in which Kant understood the necessary ethic of "practical reason".

Satyagraha

We are used to thinking of Satyagraha as a technique for social action, which Gandhi used to free India of British rule. This is true as far as it goes, but it falls short of Gandhi's intent. Satyagraha is actually a way of approach conflict and resolve it non-violently, on many levels of human interaction. Its use begins with the individual and in the home and extends to the community, to institutions, and to countries. Wherever conflict arises, subtle or violent, satyagraha has a place of importance.

As Gandhi developed it, Satyagraha is not simply a technique or theory, but a way of life. All of Gandhi's ideas bear this imprint that they achieve their potential only in their application, 'only by living them'. Gandhi did not invent Satyagraha, he discovered it;

Satyagraha, he said ' as old as the hills'. Gandhi defined its principles and applied them on as large a scale as possible to show their efficacy. But all the while he made it clear that the practice of satyagraha had to begin with the individual, 'at hope'.

Gandhi developed satyagraha with 'simple' people in mind, so that its power would be accessible to the average man and women. Satyagraha requires no higher degrees or special training, since it is founded on the most fundamental law of human nature, love. We all have the capacity for satyagraha within us, Gandhi assured us, but we do not know how to release its 'irresistible' power.

Talisman

Gandhi said, 'I will give you a Talisman. When ever you are in doubt or when the self becomes too much with you, try the following expedient: recall the face of the poorest and the most helpless man whom you may have seen and ask yourselves if the step you contemplate is going to be off any use to him. Will he be able to gain anything by it? Will it restore him to a control over his own life and destiny? In other words, will it lead to... self-rule for the hungry and also spiritually starved millions of our country men? Then you will find your doubts, and your self melting away.' (Eknath Easwran, *Gandhi the Man*, Jaico Publishing House, Mumbai, 2007, pp. 149-50)

Gospel of Service

Gandhi drew strength and inspiration from the *Bhagavad-Gita*. He says, 'the Gita contains the Gospel of work, the Gospel of Bhakti or devotion, and the Gospel of Gyan or knowledge. Life should be a harmonious whole of these three.' Gandhiji's originality lies in the great stress that he places on *Karma Yoga* (path of work). That is knows as 'Gospel of Service'. It was the guiding principle of his life and he founded to be the basis of the Gita. He says, ' the human body is meant for service, never for indulgence. Renunciation is life. Indulgence spells death'.

Service to humanity has been the ideals of all saints and prophets of peace and so it is with Gandhi. He therefore, specifically states: ' the gospel of service is the basis of all and so what can be more necessary for those who want to serve the country than that the begin with the chapter enunciating the Gospel of Work'.

Gandhi states that renunciation of the fruits of one's actions is the basic teaching of the Gita. Action is not to be avoided and cannot be avoided. For a man who follows the teachings of the Gita, sanyas is not actual renunciation of all actions. It is renunciation of the fruits of action as Gandhiji state, and it is also renunciation of the mental attachment to the fruits. Sanyas is a state of mind and the true sanyasi makes no difference between human beings. His spends his time for the betterment of all. The life Gandhiji is the history of man who became greater and nobler day by day, ultimately to become an ideal man.

The object of the Gita appears to Gandhi to be that of showing the best way to attain self-realization. What Schopenhauer said of the Upanishads – Upanishads are solace of my life, they will be a solace of death – can be said to have been accepted by Gandhiji with reference to the Gita. Thus the Gita and the ideas of Gandhi on Gita would provide some ideals and thoughts for the code of ethics for social workers.

Gandhi Seva Sangh

The initiation, deliberation and projection of all Gandhi's ideas required a forum, a group of like- minded persons themselves engaged in a variety of pursuits. This function was performed by Gandhi Seva Sangh, initially creating in 1923, to promote the programmes placed before the country by Gandhi and reconstituted and widened to include a membership of hundreds when Gandhiji made Wardha (Seva Gram) his news enter. After Gandhiji settle down in Wardha in 1934 and then moved to Seva Gram in the summer of 1936, this Gandhi Seva Sangh began to function more actively and with a much broader base. After its reorganization the first major conference, of the Sangh was held in Wardha in November 1934.

Gandhi wrote: ' the seva sangh is framing a new constitution. It has decided to incur no fresh obligations. It will enlist workers who hold common ideas without needing to have a common purse' (CW, Vol. 59. Pp.424-5, letter dated 5-12-1934 to N.R.Mulkani. These workers included writers, educationists, a scientist, technologists, medical men, social workers, analysts and scholars, and people actively engaged in the Indian National Movement against the foreign rule.Gandhiji also thought of organizing labour

in such a manner that there would be no strikes and no 'class wars' [*Hindustan Times*, 30-3-1938, p.1] Thus, during the period of 1934 till the beginning of 1940 Gandhi seems to have applied himself to thought concerning the approaches, institutions and structures which seem to be required to the functioning of the new India (Dharmapal, *Understanding Gandhi*, p.28)

Gandhi's political and economic ideals were generally considered as in practical or more gently stated, Utopian. That opinion may continue to persist well into the twenty-first century. Yet, even this view cannot be affirmed with any certitude till his ideas are examined on the basis of adequate information, knowledge, understanding and experiments. Unfortunately, this has not happened. To an extent it did not happened because India itself opted for different road. (Dharmapal, *Understanding Gandhi*, p.29).

Self-discipline

Gandhi's constant emphasis on truth and non-violence should not make one over look or ignore his other attributes. He not only had a vision of the 'desirable society' but was also a great 'law-giver' and an incomparable general. Those whom he moved to great deeds certainly had known military armaments. They were soldiers none the less. To the extent they had adequate courage, discipline and self- control, they were successful in the task they undertook. Those who joined him in his ashrams, whether in 1915 at Sabaramati or later in its innumerable prototypes in various parts of India were trained through the practice of the ashram vows which were founded on the ancient 'yama-niyama-vrathas' of India. This inevitably meant a life of austerity and hard work, and the imbibing of a sprit of brotherhood in common endeavours with others.

The task before Gandhi was note only to generate courage and confidence but also toughness and tenacity (perhaps he succeeded better with the latter two qualities) in those who came to him or listened to him at all. His own exemplary conduct, the esteem he commanded, the self -denial and discipline which even ordinary people adopted at his persuasion, and the benefits and experience gained by them in the various battles they joined under this common or approval helped toughen, train and discipline , the larger populace. To the extent this self-denial, training and toughening were deficient, they failed in their training, etc., that they would have always succeeded in what they set out to do is debatable. In such an eventuality, they would have willingly perished to the last individual and that according to him would have been success enough. The different issues which Gandhi undertook to advocate and for which, he strived seemed to have served the same the central purpose. For example, he explained that swaraj was to him like the vatavrisha (banyan tree) whose branches struck root in the earth all around it. Therefore feeding any particular branch was like feeding the whole tree, but it was even better feeding, to change the branch that was being fed from time to time.

Any change in particular and social and political change achieved through violence and force is not sustainable in the long run. The collapse of the Soviet Union and other Central and Eastern European socialist states have proved this truth. Violence debases and dehumanizes a civilized society.

To Students

Truthfulness is the master-key. Do you lie under any circumstances whatsoever. Keep nothing secret, take your teachers and elders into your confidence and make a clean breast of everything to them. Bear ill-will to none, do not say an evil thing of anyone behind his back; above all, 'to thine ownself be true' so that you are false to no one else. Truthful dealing, even in the least little things of life, is the only secret of a pure life.(*Young India*, English weekly journal edited by Mahatma Gandhi, 7-5-1931).

Let them penetrate the village and find an unlimited scope for service, research and true knowledge. Professors would do well not to burden either boys or girls with literary studies during the vacation, but prescribe to them educative outings in the villages. Vacations must be utilized for recreation, never for memorizing books. (*Young India*, English weekly journal edited by Mahatma Gandhi, 17-11-1929).

Students must devote a part of their spare time, if not the whole, to the service of thousands of Harijans..... I have found that, if I get many helpers who can give their spare time, work can be done...

This problem cannot be tackled by hired labour. No amount of money can enable me to do this. It must be your prerogative. It is an acid test of the education received by you in schools and colleges. Your worth will not be measured by your ability to make faultless English speeches. Your worth will be measured by the service you render to the poor and not by Government posts, worth Rs. 60 or Rs.600 that you may have got. (*Harijan*, 17-11- 1933)

Students cannot afford to have party politics. They may hear all parties, as they read all sorts of books, but their business is to assimilate the truth of all and reject the balance. That is the only worthy attitude that they can take. Power politics should be unknown to the student world. Immediately they dabble in that class of work, they cease to be students and will, therefore, fail to serve the country in its crisis. ... Let them, therefore, think fifty times before rejecting my advice (Press Statement, 26-01-1941)

Q. What is your goal in education when India obtains Self-rule?

A. Character- building. I would try to develop courage, strength, virtue, the ability to forget oneself in working towards great aims. This is more important than literacy; academic learning is only a means to this great end. (Re-makers of man kind, p.104)

Gandhi's Concept of Work and Culture

In the world of Gandhian thought, religion and culture are closely related to each to other. A cultured man to him was not one who strove primarily for his own artistic or intellectual satisfaction, but one who was also concerned with the welfare of others. Gandhiji sincerely believed that work and culture were intimately and inextricably related. He utterly rejected the centuries old tradition that anything connected with manual work was degrading and unworthy of a cultured man. He declared categorically: "I pride myself on calling myself a scavenger, a weaver, a spinner and farmer and do not feel ashamed that some of the things I know but indifferently. It is a pleasure for me to identify myself with the laboring classes, because without labour we can do nothing."

His devotion to work, to action, went deep into nature and stemmed from the depths of his moral consciousness. He accepted unreservedly Carlyle's high definition of work: "All true work is blessed. He who has this blessedness let him ask for no other". He put the same idea in these words.

> "Throughout 35 years of unbroken experience of public service in several parts of the world, I have not yet understood that there is anything like spiritual or moral value apart from work and action."

His whole theory of basic education was derived from this belief in the value of work. He was not prepared to concede that culture only came from books. Like Carlyle, Tolstoy, Dewey, Kershensteiner and Tagore, he was convinced that, when children and adults work with their hands at productive labour and make socially useful things, knowledge, becomes highly motivated, is joyously acquired and is better assimilated and retained. It becomes a part of the worker's personality. He did not say, as many other professional educationists were saying: Let us have academic work plus manual work in schools. He stipulated that children should learn through doing, through undertaking socially purposeful activities and be encouraged to ask questions so that they may understand what he called the why and wherefor' of things. He would have been delighted at Kershensteiner's sentence: "The education of the worker is the door to the education of the man." He did not, however, borrow his insight from the writings of great educationists of the world. It was derived directly from his contact with the people, from seeing the way they actually acquired the knowledge which they found most useful in life, and from their spontaneous reaction to their participation in practical activities. When, with his usual shocked tactics, he put it to the educational conference at Wardha in 1937 that all knowledge presented to the children must come through practical work, many traditional routine bound educationists were skeptical, if not scandalized and argued that such a system would never produce a Tagore or a Raman, or a Ray when , incidentally, Tagore's own famous educational experiment at Bolpur had anticipated some of Gandhi's basic ideas.

One great advantage of his advocacy of work as the medium of education was that some educational views which had been considered quite unacceptable, acquired a certain measure of respectability. Many persons, however, accepted , or return to accept them not because they came from the 'master' a compliment which he hardly relished. Handwork came into its own at least in theory and, to some extent in practice and long established traditions which had acquired a powerful strangle-hold on teachers as well as educational institutions, relaxed to some extent, the rigidity of their grip.

He envisaged education as 'the spherehead' of a silent 'social revolution' which might bring the urban and rural population nearer, break down the barriers between the classes and masses, provide a realistic education for both and thus lay the foundation for the just social order in which there is no un natural division between the ' haves' and 'have-nots'. All this has, of course, not been achieved but we have made some headway in this direction. As a result of the total Gandhian impact on this situation , the conflicts of interest and objectives between these two classes has tended to diminish, to some extent and there are some true Gandhian workers who continue to work, often in obscurity, for the welfare of the under privileged groups. [K.S. Saiyidain, *Significance of Gandhi as a man and thinker*, Publications Division, GOI, 2005]

Social Action and Thought

No one realized better than Gandhi the tragedy of speculative thought without social action and of social action without true reflections. Living in India, he had understood the aridity and futility of thought divorced from social action, of theory divorced from practice, of intellectual speculation divorced from pragmatic truth and from reflection anchored to concrete situations and problems. What should, therefore, attract a social scientist to Gandhi is his insistence on the primacy of rational thought as the basis of social action.

The social philosophy that sustained his life- work and life-style was as a eclectic and 'open- ended' as Gandhi himself. That is why Gandhi is so relevant to the modern world. Marx stood for an 'open- ended' system of thought. He was scared of Marxist who tried to convert it into a closed system. Gandhi was no system-builder, and yet he stood for a system of social thought which was 'open-ended' as a system. It had a clarity of design which we have to recapture in the present generation for our own enlightenment.

An 'open-ended' system of social philosophy has one essential characterstic – unity of thought and practice. The primacy of this unity was recognized by both Gandhi and Marx, but Gandhi understood it as a part of his philosophy of social action in his own characterstic fashion. He called himself a 'practical idealist' in the sense in which Kant understood the necessary ethic of 'practical reason.' He could say, in the words of Kant, 'let us seek the happiness in others, whether it bring us no happiness or pain, and so as to treat humanity, whether in thine own person or in that of another , in every case as an end, never only as a means.' Kant had said, 'to create an ideal community of rational beings we need only act as if we already belonged to it – we must apply the perfect law in the imperfect state'. Gandhi was in such of an ideal community. He tried to apply the 'the perfect law in the imperfect state', and in his own way ' to apply the eternal truths to our daily life and problems'. Gandhi had a vision of the future as an inspiring picture of the future (not a forecast based on a scientifically plausible hypothesis), or what the world would be like, if one day his ethic found the allegiance of every body. There was a element of myth in what he said or wrote in the sense that what was involved was present morality stated futuristically (a myth is ambiguous because ambiguity lies in the social facts themselves). Gandhi was thus able to lead one of the greatest mythopoeic movements of modern times.

At the same time, Gandhi was a pragmatist , who regarded himself not a visionary, but as a 'practical idealist', as one who combined moral adventure with a series of 'experiments with truth'. In 1936, he observed: 'The opinions that I have formed and the conclusions I have arrived at are not final, I may change them tomorrow. I have nothing new to teach the world. Truth and non-violence are as old the hills. All I have done is to try experiments in both on as vast a scale as possible. 'To him, his experiments with truth was even more important than his experiments with non-violence. It was this pursuit of rational Truth which imparted to his social philosophy, a quality of fascinating coherence. He was not an activist without a systematic social philosophy. It was a coherent social philosophy that gave him self-assurance not only as a vivacious controversialist, but also man of action who had to take decisions in movements of crisis.

In 1947, when Gandhi's feeble voice was in the wilderness ,

which many people did not wish to hear but which still refused to be silenced, he once spoke with the calm self assurance of a person to whom his social philosophy had revealed its unity of design just as a controversial work of art reveals the beauty of the composition to a painter.

National Education and Craft-oriented Education

The swadeshi movement of 1905- 06 threw up three seminal ideas. In retrospect they seem to have foreshadowed Gandhiji's architectonic ideas that dominated a whole generation in the entire subcontinent. These were, 1) organization of the rural masses into economically and politically self-reliant communities; 2) Passive resistances; 3) national education.

National education, as part of swadeshism, was conceived as education that was national in inspiration and methods and goals. National education, as Paul put it, 'will undertake to train up the people, the youth of the nation, in such a way as will enable them to earn an independence living, independent of government service or those professions which are under the control of the foreign government.' It followed from this objective that every boy must have compulsory technical education, which 'he must have, if not for earning bread, as least as a part of the general liberal culture; because making of things is regarded as part of liberal education. Therefore, whoever goes out of school, will have learnt something by which he earn, say Rs. 15/- or 20/- if he cannot earn more.'

Gandhi arrived on the Indian scene in 1915, a little less than a decade of after the Swadeshi movement in 1905 -06 and after this movement had petered out, leaving behind a rich legacy of ideas of national self-respect, national self reliance and organization of the masses for bread as well as freedom. It is interesting to analyze how Gandhi imbibed these ideas in his own way to build a mass base for the struggle for bread and freedom. When Gandhi visited South India in 1915, on one occasion after being presented with an address in English, he said: 'If you hold you are swadeshi and yet print this in English then I am not swadeshi.'

Gandhi was troubled by the thought of an idealness and unemployment and the lack of opportunities for work. Henry

Ford also said: 'Nothing does more to abolish poverty than worth. Everyman who works is helping to drive poverty away.' Gandhi never lost any opportunity of insisting that intellect must be combined with manual work for a more balanced kind of life. Henry Ford seemed to think likewise. Thus he said: 'No body can think straight who does not work for idealness warps the mind'. This painful aspect of mass unemployment in India troubled Gandhi most. It is a wonder that we do not here more about the fact that the practiced hand gives balance to be brain. Thinking which does not connect with the constructive action becomes a disease'. Here we become aware of the common wellspring of Henry Ford's and Gandhi's social philosophy – pragmatism in its broad sense. It was their pragmatism which moulded their similar outlook on education. Henry Ford noted the shift of emphasis to manual work in his country: 'With the changing wheel of ambition, boys no longer regard the talkative professions as more important than the manual. They realize that there are gigantic tasks to be done and that these will be accomplished by doers rather than talkers.' Gandhi similarly believed in an education which would breed doers rather than talkers and emphasized the importance of acquiring manual skills and the habit of applying one's mind to manipulative and constructive work even of the simplest kind through craft-oriented education. When people told that the Dewey system had failed in the USA, his said that it had not been tried on national scale there and that the lack of success could not be ascribed to the lack of soundness of this system.

Teaching of Hygiene and Sanitation Rules to Rural Community

In Champaran, one of the main objects of village schools that Gandhi opened, with the active participation of some of the best social workers who responded to his call, was to teach the elementary rules of hygiene and sanitation to rural communities ignorant of them. He found that landlords did not take interest in this work. While speaking of ideal land lord he, therefore said: 'He will not be satisfied with the ryots' ignorance of the laws of sanitation and hygiene ' the ideal landlord of his conception had to be a leader, not be command and exact obedience, but one who would identify himself with the poor peasants by sharing what he had with them. Thus Gandhi said: 'He will study the economic conditions of the ryots under his care, establish schools in which he will educate his own children side by side with those of the ryots. He will purify the village well and the village tank. He will teach the ryot to sweep his roads and clean his latrines himself doing this necessary labour. He will throw open without reserve his own gardens for the unrestricted use of the ryots. He will use as hospitals, school or the like, most of the unnecessary building which he keeps for his pleasure.' (B.N. Ganguli, *Gandhi's Social Philosophy Perspective and Relevance*, Council for Social Development, Vikas Publishing House, Delhi, 1973).

Summing Up

In Gandhi one comes across a remarkable fusion of social thought and social action. His life was a saga of experiments with truth. Truth that he sought resided in the human condition and in action that responded to it, actions, however, being family anchored to a value system. His social philosophy, as pieced together was a long dialogue between him and this country. It was also a dialogue between him and the world, because the Gandhi never looked at India as an entity apart from the world. if he was critical of western society and the civilization, his criticism, in so far as it was a state of tension involved in the polarity of opposites, reflected a deep concern for man wherever he happened to be. Basic education was a social thought and social action in this direction. India after independence decided not to give basic education a chance to grow and flourish.

9

The Role of Values in Education in the Context of Globalization: The Gandhian Perspective

Rama Rao Dharmana & Rajeswari Gulipilli

India is at the crossroads of development. Like all other third world countries, India faces today, the greatest of challenges in front of socio-economic development, education, health and welfare of the masses. The unprecedented population growth, unbalanced regional development and widening rural-urban disparities, increasing rate of unemployment and underemployment, malnutrition, under-nutrition, widespread of diseases and inadequate health services, an inadequate availability of safe drinking water, sanitation and poor quality of life, increasing incidences of violence against women, growing environmental degradation, pollution and the resulting eco-crisis etc., place the country at the most trying times in its history. In addition, the frequent communal strife and terrorism in the recent years, a growing regional consciousness and a threat to the national integration so on, are fast eroding away the social fabrics of the country.

Education

According to Gandhiji—"Literacy is neither the beginning nor the end of education. This is only a means through which man or woman can be educated." He believed that education should develop all the capacities of the child so that he becomes a complete human being. Complete human being means full development of body, mind, heart and soul of the child. In this way, Gandhiji advocated that education should develop the child's individuality fully and harmoniously so that he is able to realize the ultimate aim of life which is Truth or God. Gandhiji has himself explained education as—"By education I mean an all-round drawing out of the best in children and man's body, mind and spirit." Gandhiji's scheme of education is known as Basic Education. Its curriculum is activity-centred. Its aim is to prepare the child for practical work, conduct experiments and do research so that he is able to develop himself physically, mentally and spiritually and become a useful member of society. In this activity-centred curriculum, Gandhiji included Mother-tongue, Basic Craft, Arithmetic, Sociology, General Science, Art, Music and other like subjects.

Gandhiji's Philosophy of Education

Gandhiji placed the concept of Basic Education before the country in 1937. "By education I mean an all-round drawing out of the best in child and man—body, mind and spirit," he wrote in an article in Harijan in July that year and that was the beginning of the greatest experiment in the theory and practice of education in our country. He put forth ideas which had the experience of years of solid work with the masses behind them and could form the basis of a good system of education.

Gandhiji's contribution to education is unique. He was the first Indian who advocated a scheme of education based upon the essential values of Indian culture and civilization. The methods and techniques advocated by him and the environment he prescribed revolutionized Indian thinking and way of living. At heart he was devoted to Idealism. He wanted to translate his ideals and values into practice. His philosophy of education is a harmonious blending of Idealism, Naturalism and Pragmatism. It may be noted that there is no inherent conflict between the three philosophies. They are contributory to one another. Idealism is the base of Gandhiji's philosophy whereas Naturalism and Pragmatism are the helpers in translating that philosophy into practice.

Gandhiji advocated the ideals of truth, non-violence and moral values to achieve the ultimate truth of self-realization. He is a devotee of Naturalism when he speaks about the development of the child according to his nature and he becomes a Pragmatist when he advocates learning by doing and learning by experience. All these lead to an integration, so essential to effective education and development of the total personality. Dr. M.S. Patel has rightly remarked-"The real greatness of Gandhiji as an educational philosopher consists in the fact that the dominant tendencies of Naturalism, Idealism and Pragmatism are not separate and independent in his philosophy, but they fuse into a unity, giving rise to a theory of education which would suit the needs of the day and satisfy the loftiest aspirations of the human soul."

A conference of educationists from the various provinces was called at Wardha shortly after Gandhiji's articles on the subject. It was this conference which gave birth to the scheme of Basic Education under the stewardship of the Late Dr. Zakir Hussain. The following four resolutions were passed:

1. Free and compulsory education should be given to all children for a period of seven years.
2. The medium of instruction should be the mother-tongue.
3. The process of education should be centered round some form of manual, production work in the shape of a craft.
4. This education should be self-supporting to some extent.

The Central Advisory Board of Education appointed a committee under the chairmanship of Shri B.G. Kher to examine the possibilities of implementing these resolutions. This committee emphasized that the scheme was one of the education and not of production. After this another committee was appointed under the same chairman to coordinate the Basic system with higher education. The recommendations of both these committees were accepted by the Central Advisory Board of Education and incorporated in the report on Post-war Educational Development in India, published in 1944. This report was approved by the Government of India and the State Governments.

Although the Government of India and the State governments accepted Basic Education as the national pattern, it was never given a fair trial. The Kothari Education Commission 1964-66 incorporated in its recommendations many of the essential features of Basic Education. Work-experience, community living , community service, integration of academic knowledge with experience, respect for all religions and world citizenship, have been recommended by the Commission in the light of what it terms a "modernism'.

National Education Conference was convened by Shriman Narayan at Sevagram in October 1972-after a lapse of more than three decades. The Conference was inaugurated by Prime Minister Indira Gandhi. It was attended by almost all the Education Ministers and a good number of Vice-Chancellors and many eminent educationists of the country. The Conference issued a 'consensus' statement declaring that "education at all levels should be imparted through socially useful and productive activity, linked with economic growth and development in both rural and urban areas."

The Iswarbhai Patel Committee has felt that the present educational system is urban-oriented, bookish in outlook and almost entirely divorced from manual activity. In terms of opportunity, this has proved discriminatory against the poor and weaker sections of society. The Committee feels that the principles of Basic Education, as evolved by Mahatma Gandhi, and accepted in the Kothari Commission Report with the stress on work education, need to find a central place in the educational system.

The UNESCO Commission on the Development of Education, in the course of its excellent report entitled, 'Learning to be' has adopted the term Basic Education for primary education and emphasized that "education must cease being confined within school, house walls, and many forms of social and economic activity must be used for educational purposes."

The Basic Education, as originally conceived, was to cover the education of children from seven to fourteen. On the basis of experience and further thinking, Gandhiji extended both the scope and content of Basic Education. Addressing Basic Education workers at Sevagram he said that we must participate in the homes of the children. We must educate their parents. Basic Education must become literally education for life. Gandhiji explained this new conception of Basic Education as education for life and through life. He stated that the scope of Basic Education has to be extended. It should include the education of everybody at every stage of life.

Salient Features

1. Basic education is the most practical and unique contribution of Gandhiji. He placed the concept of Basic education before the country in 1937. Education Commission (1964-66) has accepted some features of Basic education as work experience, community living, integration of academic knowledge with experience, etc. The Ishwarbhai Patel Committee has also stressed that the principles of Basic education should find a central place in the educational system. Even the UNESCO Commission has adopted the term Basic education for primary education.
2. Basic education is a system of primary education from 6 to 14. Process of education centres round a craft.
3. It is an education for life and through life.
4. It is called basic because it forms its base, is based on Indian culture, comes first in time, is imparted through basic necessities of life and is linked with the basic urge.
5. The curriculum consists of a craft, mother-tongue, social studies, mathematics, general science, art, Hindi, games etc.
6. Basic education is significant as it advocates a Labour philosophy of life; work occupies a central place; advocates a new method of teaching; education is self-supporting; aims at imparting education for citizenship.
7. Basic education has not been able to make headway because selection of craft was not proper; self-sufficiency aspect has been neglected; teaching through a craft has not been taken seriously; it has turned out to be a system of education for lower classes.
8. Basic education has been hailed as a good system of primary education all over the world.

Globalization

The term 'globalization' means integration of economies and societies through cross-country flows of information, ideas, technologies, goods, services, capital, finance and people. Cross-border integration is multidimensional including cultural, social, economic and political dimensions. The International Monetary Fund defines 'globalization' as "the growing economic interdependence of countries worldwide through increasing volume and variety of cross-border transactions in goods and services and of international capital flows and also through the more rapid and widespread diffusion of technology.

Charles Hill defines 'globalization' as "the shift towards a more integrated and interdependent world economy. Globalization has two components – the globalization of markets and the globalization of productions."The process of globalization in India started with the economic reforms initiated in 1991. These economic reforms were aimed at integrating the Indian Economy with the world economy. The Narsimha Rao government, at the Centre in 1991, was forced to go in for globalization. Globalization has transformed the world into a global village. Under the provisions of the General Agreement on Trade in Services (GATS), Indian education is bound to face formidable competition from the foreign countries.

Globalization and Education Objectives

The stated objectives of globalization of education, as put forth by the proponents of globalization are:

- The motives of the foreign education providers are altruistic.
- They want to help the countries by moving into those countries.
- The foreign education providers are interested in supplying the same quality of education to the host countries that they maintain in their main campus in their own country.

That these objectives are more on paper than practice is obvious from the action that is initiated by the AICTE to regulate the growth of foreign universities and colleges in the country.

Advantages of Globalization

- Movement of the capital ensures that the total savings of the world are distributed among several countries.
- Flow of latest technologies from developed countries to the developing countries.

- Development of the capital markets takes place, as it is one of the prerequisites for the international flow of capital.
- Development of foreign exchange market is ensured, as it is one of the prerequisites for the international flow of capital.
- International trade is developed with allocation of resources in tune with the comparative advantages.
- Industrial development gets a boost because of new technologies, huge capital and managerial expertise that is made accessible to the domestic companies.
- Companies no longer depend upon markets in a particular country, as the market is worldwide.
- Cultural exchange takes place among countries making people demand a variety of products that are consumed in other countries.
- Because of the availability of products of high quality at lower prices, the consumption levels go up.
- Because of the shifting of manufacturing facilities to the low-wage developing countries, employment opportunities increase manifold.

The Impact of Globalization on Education

Threats and opportunities in the globalization of education can be assessed only when one is clear about the motives. Those who subscribe to the economic perspective of the education are the strongest proponents of globalization of education, as they believe that this process must go on concomitant with the process of economic globalization. They opine:

- The job opportunities and the needs of the economy are the driving forces for the globalization of education.
- Knowledge, skills and competency required for the vocations and professions in demand are the major focus of the globalization of education.
- All jobs, vocations and professions will acquire the same character worldwide demanding similar skills, professional competencies and knowledge.
- The work, success in career or profession is the ultimate aim of human life.

- The educational packages being offered by foreign universities and colleges being only job related have neutral value and as such cannot have negative socio-cultural psychological implications.
- Human beings are essentially self-centered and are motivated to work only for personal gain.

Taking advantage of this situation as provided by globalization, our country need to revive owe educational system keeping in view Gandhian approach and methodology which then will attract the attention of all other countries to diffuse such system in their respective countries.

We have a rich heritage of wisdom coming from ancient times in combining the secular, moral and spiritual elements in the educational process. We have also the heritage of great thought on education by great tinkers like Mahatma Gandhi, Swami Vivekananda and Pandit Nehru. Mahatma Gandhi, for instance, while emphasising education as a means of developing the potentialities of the child and his / her character, also emphasised that the social relevance of modern science and technology should be seriously considered in the context of poverty, and degradation of millions of Indian people.

The demand for value oriented education at various levels, offering package of modern knowledge and skills in various disciplines of study is based on the premise that human and spiritual values serve as powerful motivating factors for the students to grow and develop not only as an intellectual but also as a moral being, capable of playing his / her role properly in the family and society and for the material and moral progress of mankind.

As Acharya Ramamurty Committee on Education (1990) observed that the while competence to reflect on critical issues facing humanity in the spheres of social, economic or cultural life is important for the students at higher level, they have also a valuable role to play by way of participating in various national, social and cultural development programmes, such as universal literacy, health care of the poor development of backward areas and regions etc., Towards this end the curriculum and the culture, education system should be dynamically integrated with such issues and programmes. Such action oriented educational process would also help in strengthening faith in human, social and moral values.

Suggestions for Value-Oriented Reforms

It is time therefore that the educational system should give serious consideration to reconstruct our system of education in respect of value – orientation on the following lines:

1. The general education programme needs to be further strengthened and reoriented to human values and instructions in the courses of study prescribed should be spread over the entire period of study at all levels.
2. It is very necessary to continue the programmes of basic education at the lower levels of education and strengthen it further.
3. At higher level well-designed and well-organized extra curricular and extension programmes need to be organised for understanding and practice of values for the benefit of both students as well as the teachers.
4. Regular instruction in meditation and yoga practice and techniques for self development (physical, mental and moral) in the light of our Indian traditions.

Unfortunately during the last few decades, traditional extra curricular programmes have lost their importance and almost disappeared. Such actions undoubtedly by provide valuable learning experiences and organisational skills for students and support their intellectual, social and moral development. It is necessary therefore to review these actions in the interests of value-orientation of education. Whatever attempts are made in this direction by both proper participation by the students and faculty as well as management.

10

Youth and Global Peace in Gandhian Perspective

P. Kishore Kumar & B. Chennaiah

The entire humanity has been craving for peace at different levels such as individual, social, communal, national and international levels. Attainment of peace should be the ultimate goal of any youthful human emotions and actions. Once their minds are at rest they can concentrate their energies for spreading the message of peace. Youth should know that social harmony is an index of peace. They should strive peacefully to make their and other people's social lives happy and undisturbed which is the aim of any society. All the religions have preached peace and harmony. The advocacy of war was for the purpose of saving the religion, performing one's duty and eliminating the veils so that society can enjoy a happy and peaceful life. Gandhiji was of the view that peace is a feeling which is to be emotionally experienced by everyone. It is experienced when emotional equilibrium and self-equalization is achieved. It is this superpower, he felt, which if realized, leads to eternal happiness.

Gandhiji also warned youngsters against misinterpreting religions. All the religions such as Hinduism, Christianity, Islam, Buddhism, Jainism, etc. have preached peace and harmony. The advocacy of war was for the purpose of saving the religion, performing one's duty and eliminating the veils so that society can enjoy a happy and peaceful life. Mahatma Gandhi himself made skillful use of Satyagraha to achieve peace and harmony and thus proved his point. He always believed that peace contains a negative and a positive sense; the absence of configuration, elimination of wars, absence of conflicts between different classes, castes, religions, and nations is a negative sense and love, rest, mental equilibrium, harmony, co-operation, unity, happiness are the positive indices of peace.

Gandhiji's Views on Youth as an agent for community renovation

"What is my inheritance? To what am I an heir? To all that humanity has achieved during tens of thousands of years, to all that is has felt and suffered and taken pleasure in, to its cries and triumphs and its bitter agony of defeat, to that astonishing adventure of man which began so long ago and yet continues and beckons to us.

To all this and more in common with all men. But there is a special heritage for those of us of India, not an exclusive one, for none is exclusive and all are common to the race of man, one more especially applicable to us, something that is in our flesh and blood and bones, that has gone to make us what we are and what we are likely to be...an agent....an agent for community renovation!

Today we are here to present our research on Gandhiji's views on youth as an agent for social transformation. Even as we sit here in this gathering peacefully little do we know that there is a war being waged. A war where the youth of nation will actively participate...a war of good vs. evil, a war of virtues vs. vices, a war of knowledge of science vs. wisdom of soul, a war of material prosperity vs. peace of mind, a war of education vs. character building, a war of professional management vs. social commitment.

The lines for battle have been drawn and this battle will be fought on three fronts:

- The Environment front,
- The Social front, and
- The Individual front.

This will indeed be a unique battle where everyone will emerge as a winner. What are the weapons to be used in this war? Right Conduct, Love, Cooperation, Justice, Equality, Patriotism, Non-Violence, Peace, Excellence and last but not the least, the all powerful weapon of Truth. The able-bodied soldiers namely the youth of India are being lead by none else but our beloved Mahatma as the Commander-in-chief.

Let us take a closer look at the various strategies that we shall be using in this war and how we shall tackle the enemy on each front. One important factor to be remembered is that this battle started nearly a hundred years ago when the Mahatma himself fought in the ranks of a soldier and continues till date. It is important to know the history of this war before we decide what tactics are to be adopted in the future. Hence we need to visit each of the warfronts to get a better idea.

The Environmental Front

Let us deal with this battlefield in a Gandhian manner by incorporating the two vital issues of Peace and Patriotism. Right from the beginning of human life, the entire humanity has been craving for peace at different levels such as individual, social, communal, national and international levels. Gandhiji was of the view that peace is a feeling which is to be emotionally experienced by everyone. It is experienced when emotional equilibrium and self-equilisation is achieved. It is this superpower, he felt, which if realised, leads to eternal happiness. Attainment of peace should be the ultimate goal of any youthful human emotions and actions. Once their minds are at rest they can concentrate their energies for spreading the message of peace. Youth should know that social harmony is an index of peace. They should strive peacefully to make their and other people's social lives happy and undisturbed which is the aim of any society. Gandhiji also warned youngsters against misinterpreting religions. All the religions such as Hinduism, Christianity, Islam, Buddhism, Jainism, etc. have preached peace and harmony. The advocacy of war was for the purpose of saving the religion, performing one's duty and eliminating the veils so that society can enjoy a happy and peaceful life. Mahatma Gandhi himself made skillful use of Satyagraha to achieve peace and harmony and thus proved his point. He always believed that peace contains a negative and a positive sense; the absence of configuration, elimination of wars, absence of conflicts between different classes, castes, religions, and nations is a negative sense and love, rest, mental equilibrium, harmony, co-operation, unity, happiness are the positive indices of peace.

In broader sense, peace would include social harmony which involves natural resources. Gandhiji believed that natural resources are the primary sources for valuable and useful commodities. They are mainly raw materials and energy resources present in the environment. e.g. minerals, forest, animals, water, soil. Youth should ensure its proper utilisation and conservation. This would imply rational use of resources and their preservation from reckless exploitation and destruction. Gandhiji's love for animals is known to all. He further advocated effective control and management of resources in such a way that they will be useful to man for longer time. He underlined young student's importance in ensuring uniform distribution of all resources.

In the same context of environment another weapon that Gandhiji has provided us with is Patriotism. The nation, he emphasised, is built on the foundation of selfless devotions by its citizens. Young people are vibrant, energetic and enthusiastic. They should show the same enthusiasm when the nation demands for sacrifice of their wealth, their lives, their families etc. Gandhiji often recited a verse in Sanskrit stating that Mother and Motherland are superior to Heaven. He went to the extent of coining his own definition of Patriotism wherein he described it as a sense of loyalty and affection to the soil, the national symbols etc. This feeling, sentiment or attitude of patriotism, he believed would make youth serve the nation selflessly.

Social Front

History has numerous instances of old and well-established civilizations fading away or being ended suddenly, and vigorous new cultures taking their place. It is some vital energy, some inner source of strength that gives life to civilization or people without which all efforts are ineffective, like the vain attempt of an aged person to play the part of a youth? Such was the vitality attached to young students by our beloved Father of the Nation!

So what is this social transformation that he was referring to using youth as a catalyst? Society, as defined, is a group of individuals dwelling together who symbiotically carries out various activities to bring happiness and stabilization. As it is a unique blend of diverse religions, cultures, and races its structure keeps changing with respect to time. After all, nothing is constant but "change"! Gandhiji had stressed upon youth participation in bringing out various social reforms during his struggle for independence in the Sati Pratha, Polygamy, Child marriage, Education of women, Widow remarriage, Untouchability, Caste system, Exploitation and Religious misguidance. And the attributes that make youth swim through were Non-violence, Co-operation, Justice, Equality and Love. Non-violence, Gandhiji advocated, has a religious, social, spiritual and personal significance. Force or aggression leads to a total destruction of society. Violent feelings provoke conflicts which grow in strength and threaten the very society it was initially supposed to protect. As violence or force grows in size it takes a negative and destructive path and affects society. The only force, Mahatma Gandhi proposed was fasting which could be coercive but upright. The path proposed was of Non-cooperation, boycott or Satyagraha. Let us not forget that satyagraha was the subtle force which he used to shake the very foundation of the British Empire! He believed in the destruction of the false and the wicked by non-violence which would eventually result in the ultimate triumph of good over all evil.

Gandhiji described the term co-operation as all individuals coming together to achieve the designed goals and all of them sharing the fruits of the achievements. Nobody is overburdened nor over regarded. Youth should co-operate with elders and children. It should be looked upon as a way of life. "Vina Sahakar Nahi Uddhar" (No prosperity without co-operation). He underlined that co-operation is the basis for peace, love, equality and justice. Mahatma Gandhi advocated joint families and village communities as the cooperation among different individuals, classes, castes and groups in the society ensures growth in all walks of human life from basic needs of food clothing and shelter to more complex requirement of the people like industries, transportation, recreation, finance etc. Gandhiji also proposed the young entrepreneurs concept to achieve primary objectives of growth and equality. Gandhiji wanted youth against the misuse of Co-operation like undue publicisation, excessive government intervention, exploitation, promotion of self-interest etc.

Love, as per the Mahatma, is a feeling or sentiment which originates in the soul. Love for young people is a form of energy which would charge them every now and then. The entire structure of society is built upon a sound foundation of love. He advocated love strongly as it develops co-operation and a sense of understanding that makes the entire society happy. Equality, in youth, is a noble, desirable and valuable principle. A comparison between two individuals, groups, societies, natures etc. is against the natural Law, said Mahatma. After all everyone is equal in the eyes of God. Is it logical, leave alone ethical to say that one person is superior to another? Accordingly Gandhiji appealed youngsters to strive towards nullifying the wide gap between various sections of the society. He proposed elimination of all sorts of artificial discrimination, exploitation and oppression to establish equality. Men and Women are equal. They complement each other through the different functions they person in a society. He once stated that "If we do not efface untouchability we shall all be effaced from the face of the Earth". Caste, he felt does not connote superiority or inferiority. It simply recognizes difference in outlooks and corresponding modes of life.

He proposed youth to provide equal protection and security to all. Economic inequality implying concentration of wealth and income in few hands is the root cause of political instability and social inequality. He further suggested abolition of exploitation, forced labor, sexual discrimination so as to restore social harmony. Untouchability, according to him was an offence it was one of those evils which plagued society, a crime against not only humanity but against God. Unity and Equality were their core values on which a nation rests.

About justice he said that there exists a close relationship between equality and justice. Youth must know that justice is done when equality is established and when equality exists justice is done. Justice is natural or Godly ensuring the balance in the universe through young exercisers. Young people should treat justice in all fronts morel, social, political, economic. Justice is normative connotation depending upon the accepted morals of the society the predictions and customs instituted by the society for betterment of all. What is more important for youth is spreading the light of justice and creating awareness.

Individual Front

The third warfront where the war is being fought is individual level. i.e. the young mind itself. Here Gandhiji advocated the principles of Right Conduct. Excellence and Truth as the effective weapons with which to fight this war. Gandhiji was himself a disciple of the "Bhagwad Gita" and exalted the younger generation to follow it too. The Gita mentions three different qualities viz. Satva, Rajas and Tamas.

In case of Tamas the happening comes from violence and laziness. In case of Rajas it comes from material gains. Gandhiji proposed that the youth follow the Satvik model where happiness is inward development, i.e. it emphasizes the inclusion of basic human values. Right conducts refers to a set of norms or code of conduct accepted by the society on the basis of thoughtful behavior and is displayed when we discharge our duties and various actions such as obedience, etiquettes, fulfillment of social obligations, co-operation, sympathy etc. The youth should take into consideration various dimensions of their conduct such as the social, cultural, religious and the political aspect. Especially in young people, there is a constant flow of energy. They are dynamic, vibrant and excessively energetic. Hence it becomes all the more necessary for them to discharge their energies in a positive manner to attain long-term happiness and goodwill in society and to contribute to the progress of society. Gandhiji often reiterated the Hindu philosophy of Moksha or Salvation. According to him a Sadachari-a person with right conduct is ensured a place in heaven, while it is believed that a sinner will go to hell. He therefore stressed on Truth, Humanity, Sacrifice and Non-avarices the important element of right conduct. Right conduct, he believed, comes from the right education and education should not only help gain knowledge, but should also contribute towards character building. Gandhiji often referred to that one should do his duty and remain unconcerned about the fruits.

Gandhiji also pointed out that each one of us should strive to attain excellence at the personal as well as the social level. He implored the youth to pursue this value without any reservations. This would ensure not only holistic development of the individual, but also progress of the society at large. Here Gandhiji makes a reference to our age-old scriptures where Dharma, Artha, Kama and Moksha have been mentioned as the four Purusharthas, the pursuit of which leads to perfection in all walks of human life. He strongly believe in the adage that if any job is worth doing, it is worth doing well. Excellence in any field brings peace of mind and satisfaction. According to him the age-old concept life being divided into four stages or ashrams, contributed to an individual's attaining excellence.

Brahmacharyashram	- Learning
Grihaprasthashram	- Household responsibilities
Vanaprasthashram	- Living in forest away from household life
Sanyasprashthashram	- Complete freedom from material bondages and Devotion to God

Only if a person adhered strictly to these stages then his life would become worthwhile. Truth was Gandhiji's favorite human value which inspired his autobiography "My Experiments with Truth" Satya Meva Jayate was his slogan. This is as human value which leads to non-existence to human race. Youth must differentiate between truth and blind belief. Gandhiji wanted every individual and society to practice truth at any cost. He emphasized that all religions, philosophies, societies have unambiguously advocated truth. According to him truth was God and that truth must manifest itself in the thought, word and deeds. He did accept the path of truth will always be full of hardship, difficulties, sufferings, and sacrifice. To tell the truth one must be courageous. Youth must note that no society readily accepts any social transformation. Hence the students who are acting as agent for reformation will have to face public censure and the wrath of society. Self-determination, strong will power and profound belief in one's conviction will help the youth to lead the society. Trading the path of truth is a continuous and unending process which has to be followed by every generation.

Gandhiji advocated that education was the means to attain virtues. Basic education was every person's right. Children should not only learn to read and write, they must also learn some family skills, usage of which will make them independent and self-reliant. Basic education should be made compulsory for all Children upto the age of fourteen. The medium for education should be one's mother tongue, so that they can easily grasp it. Education should not end with childhood and adult education plays an equally vital role in the development of an individual.

Conclusion

Thus on all fronts Gandhiji believed in creating from youth a cadre of inspiring and competent role models and change agents with the courage of conviction who in turn will trigger off the process of building a healthy nation. The war started over 100 years ago and remains incomplete as we fight it even today. Social transformation must be undertaken on apriority and this is nothing less than a revolution. Long term fundamental changes and not merely outward changes are required. Civil cleansing and mass action is the key to this change and the youth are the catalysts who will bring about the change. The entire system needs revamping and the young people will play an instrumental role. The challenge before us to build a good society out of bad individuals.

The weapons he gave were not just meant to overthrow the British but to be used at all times. Today we require these weapons more than ever to build a better society. Even after 60 years of freedom we are still struggling to gain independence in the true sense; to pull ourselves out of the clutches of violence, crime and corruption which have rendered our entire society sick. Although free from foreign rule, we are still enchained by foreign influences which are corrupting our youth and driving them astray. The very agents of communal renovation are engulfed by the fatal diseases of poverty, illiteracy, over-population and unemployment. The time is ripe for an uprising and we must all awaken and revolt; a non-violent but effective war needs to be waged keeping in mine all that the great Mahatma taught us years ago. As we progress into the next millennium, we need to carry forward his ideologies with us.

REFERENCES

1. Charles F. Andrews, *Mahatma Gandhi: His Life and Ideals,* Jaico Publishing House, Mumbai, 2005.
2. M.K. Gandhi, *To Students,* Navajivan Publishing House, Ahmedabad, 1953.
3. Mohit Chakrabarti, *The Gandhian Philosophy of the Spinning Wheel,* Concept Publishing Company, New Delhi, 2000
4. M.K. Gandhi, *My Non-Violence,* Navajivan Publishing House, Ahmedabad, 1960
5. APJ Abdul Kalam, YS Rajan, *India 2020: A Vision for the New Millennium,* Penguin Books, 1998.

11

Globalisation: A Gandhian Perspective

K. Visweswara Rao & K. Ananda Rao

In a world plagued by the proliferation of weapons of mass destruction, menace of global terrorism, global warming and climate change, owing to environmental destruction and ecological imbalances, global epidemics like HIV/AIDS, and growing incidence of poverty related death as fallout of liberalization, privatization, and globalisation (LPG), Gandhi as well as his philosophy appears relevant forever in the area of globalization. Gandhian spirit of love, truth, non-violence, amity and unity across the globe and remind us, Gandhi is still capable to remain in the core of their heart. The statement made by Nobel Peace prize winner Desmond Tutu on the occasion of accepting "Gandhi International Peace Prize" further reaffirmed his relevance when he admits that he got the Nobel prize for Peace by following Gandhiji philosophy and wishes to dedicate it to him as he is the real winner of any peace prize around the globe and the relevance of his philosophy got wider perspective with the UN resolution on June 15, 2007 to declare commemorate 2nd October, Gandhiji's birthday as the "International Day for Non-Violence". In fact it is a big tribute as well as recognition of the relevance of Gandhian philosophy in today's trouble torn world (Dillip Kumar Maharana and Debendra Mahalik, 2007). Against this background, this paper examines the relevance of Gandhian philosophy on globalization and the relationship of globalization with the five "Ps", namely Population, Poverty, Pollution, Proliferation of armaments and Peace of the world.

Importance of being Gandhiji

The name Mohandas Karamchand Gandhi or Mahatma Gandhi does not confine to a personality only. Gandhi is more that a name. Gandhi does not mean a particular person but a way of life in India. It is a thinking known as Gandhism, which inspired every Indian to pursue for freedom with peaceful manner as well as to achieve self- sufficiency economically, politically and socially. Though he alone did not brought freedom to our country, he injected his Satyagraha and ahimsa or Non-violence to the people, which were spread like wildlife all over India. Gandhi was a miracle; he was magician without the art of magic. He thought the people how to endure the British tyranny and strike at the right time. He was not only a freedom fighter or a politician; he was simultaneously a lawyer, an educationist, a theologist, a dietician, a journalist, an economist, a litterateur and above all a social reformer (Pradosh Kumar Rath, 2002).

Gandhian Approach

Gandhian approach to socio economic development stands our distinctively different in comparison with the other two main approaches viz. of capitalism and socialism. Basically, most of the contemporary economies are, by and large characterised by centralized mode of production and either centralized or decentralized mode of distribution. In sharp contrast, Gandhian approach is based on decentralised mode of production as well as distribution. The capitalistic mode of production includes both capitalist system in which ownership over the means of production mainly vests in individuals or a group who are governed mainly by profit motive and socialist system in which ownership over the means of production vets in society and is governed by social motive. The mixed economies depending upon the intensity in ownership can be included in either of the two. But basically all the three capitalist, socialist and mixed economic system are highly capital intensive (Panditrao, 2002).

Globalisation and Gandhian Perspectives

Mahatma Gandhi has seldom written about strictly modern process of globalisation. He could not because present-day globalisation was far away in his own time. He has still reflected on related areas of international federation, world peace, exploitation of the weak by the stronger nation, freedom, equality, and dignity of the individual, primacy of the individual in a socio-political system, mechanisation, media and trade etc. As such, Gandhi has a vision for unity of mankind, universal brotherhood and "living association of human beings" the world over. Similarly, contemporary globalisation encompasses phenomenological paradigmatic evolution of technological trends from the late-nineteenth to twenty-first century in the fields of information, communication, multi-media, trade, commerce, finance, international institutions / relations, national development, political systems, and ecological patterns etc. A common special feature of these predispositions anent globalisation is the apparent unity of mankind found, among others, in the "coming together" of even distant nations through technology regulated regimes of internet, satellites, supersonic jets, multinational corporations and constantly receding international trade barriers. The modern surging ahead in multi-media technology is bringing in its wake a global transformation. Entire world has now become a "Global Village" (Patil and Gopal, 2002).

International organisations and kindred activity towards common global ends of sharing, knowing and coming together through mutual excellence are manifest processes of "globalisation". The "Global Village" phenomenon is obviously an integral part of globalisation. Marshall McLuhan coined this term "Global Village" in 1960s to express his belief that electronic communication would unite the world by brining together diverse cultures and distant people of the world. Therefore, global village does not really represent the "shrinking of the world" but widening of the electronic instantaneous communication network for brining people into togetherness. Nearly, all information and communication rests upon the click of a "mouse". Globally established really open society without any walls is in the "offing". This Global Village is very different from the decentralised village-based economy and polity preferred by India's Father of the Nation.

The prospects of present-day globalisation in the Gandhian traditions of thought and practice are not very difficult to see today. A few quotations from Gandhi's writings may help open Platonic "shadows of the cave" as it were. Writings and sayings of Mahatma

Gandhi and majority of commentators and critics of Gandhian philosophy have shown not only inherent but also explicit significance of the idea of oneness of humanity, individual's dignity and self-reliance for Swaraj in Gandhi's practical-idealist perspective of politics. Gandhi has never regarded himself as a system builder. His experiments, however, have led him to evolve– for several commentators and analysts like S.C. Gangal, Mahendra Kumar, Raghavan Iyer, Savita Singh, Ramjee Singh, Johan Galtung and others – a Predominantly Non-violent State as his second best Ideal and a Nonviolent Society as his ultimate Ideal for establishing a vibrantly creative global and just political ethos where cooperation, equality and non-violence has replaced exploitation, inequality and bloody warfare and mutual hatred. Similar ideas are currently being propagated and discussed by internationally acclaimed authors and statesmen alike even if they are apparently not so much directly influenced by Gandhi.

Gandhi's concept of holistic process of globalisation is a practical-idealist concept. Gandhi called himself a practical-idealist. Gandhi has never written or said much about globalisation in particular as a term with specific meaning that is being attached to it currently. Yet he had foreseen almost all major trends and strands of globalisation today in a positive and creative mould. For him: It is impossible for one to be an internationalist without being a nationalist. Our nationalism can be no peril to other nations in as much as we will exploit none just as we will allow none to exploit us. Decentralisation of political and economic power, reduction in the functions and importance of State, growth of voluntary associations, removal of dehumanising poverty and resistance to injustice will bring life within the understanding of man and make society and the State democratic. The non-violent State will cooperate with an international organisation based on nonviolence. Peace will come not merely by changing the institutional forms but by regenerating those attitudes and ideals of which war, imperialism, capitalism and other forms of exploitation are the inevitable expressions (Gangal, 1960).

The current movement towards Globalisation also appears to be having a number of APPARENT Gandhian values such as: 1) global unity and integration 2) fast growing antipathy to mass-violence (at least in principle on a wider plain) specially in the aftermath of the terrorist attack on New York's trade centre on 11 September 2001, 3) an evidently receding trend in ideological clashes among nations (specially between liberalism and socialism), 4) globally expanding mosaic of acceptance of the Gandhian principle of nonviolence among nations and their leaders (see specially India's response and patience to terrorist violence and attacks) and 5) end of or doing away with "war as an instrument of national policy" at least among countries of the European Union. In this age of Globalisation and increasing regional cooperation, the ideas and principles of Gandhiji are as follows:

Sustainable Development

The first and foremost point according to Gandhiji's ideas continue to be relevant in his idea about development. When the whole world is crying for the mercy to get rid of current state of environmental degradation in the form of depletion of ozone layer, global warming and climate change, Gandhiji's very notion of development appears as a savior to the world community. Sustainability is the core to his developmental process which appears to be a best viable alternative model of development in the recent years. The concept of sustainable development becomes indispensable to the development of the human civilization because of the limited nature of the world's resources. Knowing this inherent limitation of mother earth Gandhi warned the human society not to exploit beyond of its capacity to withstand the exploitation of natural resources for our development.

Self-Sufficiency

His concept of bread labour further strengthens the notion of sustainable development when says, "If all laboured for the bread and no more, then there would be enough food and enough leisure for all. There will be no rich no poor, no high, no low, no touchable and no untouchable". Therefore, it is the need of the hour to follow his notion of development rather going astray in following the destruction model of development.

Gram Swaraj

Although after the 73rd Constitutional Amendment Act efforts were made to decentralize the powers to the Gram Panchayats, yet we have to go a long way to realize the actual dream of Gandhi's

'Gram Swaraj". The fundamental concept of Gram Swaraj is that every village should be its own republic, "independent of its neighbours for its own vital wants and yet inter-dependent for many others in which dependence is necessary," according to Gandhi, writing in 1942. Each village should be basically self-reliant, making provision for all necessities of life-food, clothing, clean water, sanitation, housing, education and so on, including government and self-defense, and all socially useful amenities required by a community. The virtues of "small is beautiful" are always preferred by Gandhi as he visualized the future of India lies in the development of these small villages.

Fighting against Global Menace

In the era of global terrorism, Nuclear Weapon and Weapons of Mass Destruction, the only philosophy or rather way of life that ensures our longevity on earth is Gandhian thought of non-violence. Humanity survived amid the conflict in Stone Age, Iron Age, gun powder age, warship age and also in bomber planes age, but it is really difficult to survive in nuclear and chemical weapon age. It only needs a pull of the nuclear trigger to wipe every trace of life from this earth, and turn it into a nuclear wasteland. Today with irresponsible, fragmented and fanatical regimes acquiring nuclear capabilities and delivery systems, how will we create a world where nuclear or any other deterrent becomes unnecessary? It will only come about when we adopt Nonviolence as our creed, our way of life. Gandhi ridiculed the ideas of war to end the war. He maintained wars do not end anything except humanity. Therefore, if humanity is to survive, we must go back to Gandhi and bring peace to the 21st century.

Universalisation of Primary Education

Today India is dreaming big to be a developed country in the nearest future. Therefore, the base must be strengthened first by putting extra emphasis on Human Resource Development in terms of providing education and training to the people. Education is the main engine of growth that turns the potential power to real one. Gandhiji regarded education as the light of life and the very source from which was created an awareness of oneness. Gandhiji's education is all about drawing the best in the child and man. Gandhian way of education put emphasis on the development of body, mind, heart and soul. He believes in an education that liberates human being by imparting the kind of knowledge as a training that is useful for the service of mankind. His scheme of education called Nai Talim: a beautiful blend of Craft, Art, Health and education in one and covers the whole education of the individual for the time of conception to the moment of death. Today, the government is taking serious steps to improve the craft based education is nothing but the acceptance of Gandhiji.

Sex Education

In the world of growing menace of HIV/AIDS and other Sexually Transmitted Diseases, it would be a great shield if we all will follow the Gandhian path on education. Sex education which he called Sexual Science is of two kinds that which is used for controlling or overcoming the sexual passion, and that which is used to stimulate and feed it. He preferred sex education as science of conquest and sublimation of the sex passion. He says instruction in the former is as necessary a part of child's education while latter is harmful and dangerous and fit therefore only to be shunned.

Empowering Women

Another debated topic in which Government of India as well as the non-government organisations and inter-governmental organizations including the UN is taking interest is 'Women empowerment". But it is true that the real development of society is neither possible nor desirable by leaving half of the population in dark and depression. Realizing this virtue Gandhi advocated for the "Women empowerment". But, supporting women empowerment he writes, "of all the evils for which man has made himself responsible, none is so degrading, so shocking or so brutal as his abuse of the better half of humanity to me, the female sex, not the weaker sex. It is the nobler of the two, for it is even today the embodiment of sacrifice, silent suffering, humility, faith and knowledge. Therefore, he was in favour of educating women and giving them all freedom which men enjoy.

Communal Harmony

Today the world is witnessing more communal clashes across the globe. Even some people like Huntington is justifying it as a

"Clash of Civilization" and so inevitable. Gandhi never wished to see the people to be a communal bigot rather he pleaded for the humanization of knowledge for immunization against the ideas of distrust among the communities of the nations and the nationalities of the world. He wanted to take the country from areas of hostility into areas of harmony of faiths. He valued communal harmony and asked the people to tolerate other community as their brothers and sisters. He insisted to give the communal harmony highest priority as a key to its progress and national integration.

Prospective Challenges of Globalisation in Gandhian Approach

On the basis of the above-mentioned information, an attempt is being made to evolve a Gandhian strategy for prospective road to globalisation especially in the light of quite a few existing relatively harmful trends and patterns. Gandhi is one with former United States (US) President Bill Clinton's statement: "the central reality of our time is that the advent of globalisation and the revolution in information technology have magnified both the creative and destructive potential of every individual, tribe and nation on our planet."

Gandhi has a holistic approach to human problems, in which reform or reconstruction should concentrate, more or less at the same time, at all levels of human existence and activity, i.e. individual, local, national and international levels. Globalisation is an ever-accelerating trend of modern "civilisation".

Real globalisation for Gandhi is possible only through Panch yama of Patanjali, i.e., non-violence, non-stealing, truth, non-possession and chastity. Global though sectoral reformation programme for regeneration of every individual is needed for balancing the negative effects of the process of globalisation. It was Gandhi's conviction that individuals – of whom the nations and global communities are constituted – must have priority in any scheme of reform or reconstruction. Yet another idea in Gandhi's scheme is that any durable programme of reconstruction must be marked by a measure of coordination and integration at various levels of social action through voluntary effort. Press and media have a very significant role in this sphere. Media, for Gandhi, must be having unmistakable autonomy and self-reliance with little dependence on advertisement revenue. The cultivation of non-violence by the individual and the establishment of non-exploitative economy at different levels will lead eventually to the emergence of what he calls nonviolent nationalism. Ultimately, these nonviolent nations will function under a world federation or international organisation on the basis of:

a) Political and economic independence without any type of colonialism or imperialism and exploitation.
b) Voluntary effort with dedication and commitment.
c) Goals and means not imposed from above but developed from within.
d) Equality for all. As such every nation must feel as tall as the tallest.
e) Decentralisation at political and economic spheres.
f) General disarmament.
g) Unilateral disarmament.
h) International society as a voluntary organisation.
i) Common good of all.
j) Bigger nations ready to "give" to the smaller nations.
k) Amicable and peaceful settlement of all disputes.
l) Small international police as long as the world is able to develop a general belief in nonviolence.
m) Free, open, alert and impartial Media.
n) Preponderance to mutual sense of service.

Such a blue print should be the guiding spirit of present-day globalisation. In this pattern of globalisation, the individual has specially a two-fold significance for Gandhi. First, proper education and training to the individual for understanding and imbibing the values of a normal society. A normal fraternity, for Gandhi, is one where development does not pose diverse types of threats to the individual and humanity. For evolving such a normal course of life for true globalisation, a Global Education Order must be established through value-related and need based education. Nearly all aspects of human life are to be covered in this programme ranging from material, moral, emotional and cultural to spiritual needs of the individual. The individuality, creativity, identity and voluntary efforts have to be the fundamental terms of reference in the launching of such a global education order. Secondly, Gandhi emphasises the role of the individual in decision-making and in sharing the national and international responsibilities. There is no place for undemocratic or authoritarian regimes in Gandhi's agenda for globalisation. To steer clear of undemocratic or authoritarian tendencies, Gandhi suggests two more correctives of (i) limited State power and (ii) socio-economic decentralisation. As regards the former, Gandhi is one with Thoureau's principle that "that government is best which governs the least."

To quote Gandhi: I look upon an increase in the power of the state with the greatest fear because...it does the greatest harm to mankind by destroying individuality which lies at the root of all progress. In order to curb emergence of authoritarianism, the size and role of police and military, for Gandhi, has to be limited to dealing with thieves, robbers, raiders from without and a few emergencies only. It would be better if police and military perform largely the role of a body of reformers. Gandhi looks forward to the emergence of a world where "no state has its military."

Socio-economic decentralisation is yet another corrective measure to curb undemocratic tendencies. Gandhi's global vision moves upward from the individual and a federation of village republics to an international federation of nations in a society marked by voluntary cooperation and decentralisation. Aldous Huxley, while supporting Gandhi, says, "Democratic principles cannot be effectively put into practice unless authority in a community has been decentralised to the utmost extent possible."

The modern inter-linking of people and economies under contemporary globalisation must give careful attention to the Gandhian pointers in this age of technology for keeping away from the pejorative aspects of concurrent science and development patterns. Otherwise, globalisation will prove to be a "nine days wonder" only (Raghavan Iyer, 1986).

REFERENCES

1. David P. Brash and Charles P. Webel (2002). *Peace and Conflict Studies*, California, Sage, 5.
2. Dillip Kumar Maharana and Debendra Mahalik (2007). 'Relevance of Gandhiji in 21st Century', *Kurukshetra*, October, Vol.55, No.12, 64-68

3. Gangal, S.C. (1960). *The Gandhian Way to World Peace*, Bombay, Vora, 90.
4. Panditrao, Y.A (2002). 'Relevance of Mahatma Gandhi in the Modern Context', *Khadigramodyog*, September, Vol.XXXXVIII, No.12, 368-375.
5. Patil, V. A., and Gopal, D. (2002). *Politics of Globalisation*, Delhi, Authors Press, 01 – 11.
6. Pradosh Kumar Rath (2002). 'The Importance of being Gandhiji', *Khadigramodyog*, October, Vol.XXXXIX, No.1, 9-15.
7. Raghavan Iyer (1986). *The Moral and Political Writings of Mahatma Gandhi: Truth and Non-violence*, London, Oxford University Press, Volume – II, 181.
9. Ram K. Vepa (1975). *New Technology: A Gandhian Concept*, New Delhi, 170.

12

Relevance of Gandhian Principles for Sustainable Management of Natural Resources

P. Usha & S. Pulla Rao

In the context of the present scenario of global environmental problems, one should rely on Gandhian philosophy in managing the natural resources and there by protecting our environment from the degradation. The World Bank Report says that despite India's strong policy framework and some successes, environmental degradation has not been arrested on a large scale. India's environmental institutions and regulatory regime need to be significantly upgraded, in order to sustain rapid economic growth and meet surging public demand for a cleaner and healthier environment. Nature or environment needs to be carefully preserved failing which leads to consequences like global warming, damage of ozone layer and loss of biodiversity would play havoc with human life. In fact, Gandhiji had forecasted the threat to resources a century ago and advocated the need for sustainable management of resources and suggested how could be the resources managed in sustainable manner for the future benefit.

Keeping Gandhian principles in view, the current research paper focused on the need to manage of environment on the lines of Gandhian ideology for sustainable development. In this context, an effort is made to find out a solution to current environmental problems by making a study/referring to Gandhiji's views on ecology and man's relation with nature. No doubt that, Gandhiji's ideology and advocacies are more relevant to present day's environmental problems which are mainly due to human activities.

When we analyze the reasons for the prevailing environmental problems we may find out over population growth is one of the reasons and which ultimately demand for more goods and services and causes depletion of natural resources. Not only that the increased human consumption of resources has negative impact on the ecological services and hence it needs wise management of environment. The alarming rate of decreasing natural resources is reflected in the classical statement of natural resources by Harold Hotelling words that "contemplation of the world's disappearing supplies of minerals, forests and their exhaustible assets has led to the demand for regulation of their exploitation". It clearly reveals that over exploitation of natural resources as compared to its incremental and regenerative capacities escalates the resource depletion .of the natural resources. In other words for sustainable management of resources , the rate of consumption of resources should not exceed the rate of regenerative and equivalent development of renewable substitutes and the waste generation should not exceed the assimilative capacity of environment.

Gandhi opined that human greediness and reckless consumption of resources causes depletion of natural resources. Nature provides vital goods and services which are essential ingredients for the survival of humans and satisfy their wants But people because of their greediness and thoughtless actions have been over exploiting the natural resources and disturbing the ecological balance by destroying the nature through economic activities. The demand for more goods and services lead to pollution failing which causes climate change. Not only that, increasing urbanization pollutes clean water resources hence there is a need to emphasize proper management of water resources in order to preserve the ecological services. The underlying ecological problem of loss of biodiversity has become a great threat for the survival of human beings and other organisms.

The existing global environmental problems draws the attention of the environmentalists and policy-makers in finding solutions to reduce the intensity of the problem. In these circumstances, Gandhian vision of a 'non-violent eco-friendly world' has to be ardently followed in view of deterioration of natural resources assuming alarming proportions. As excessive use of natural resources has not only local problem it also leads to environmental degradation and negatively affect sustainable socio-economic developmental processes in the developing countries. The concept of sustainable development as defined by Brundtland Commission implies that, the future generation should not be deprived of natural resources. Hence steps should be taken to conserve the resources for sustainable society. The Caring of Earth (1991) paper of UN agencies has set out the guidelines for sustainable society. One of the most important principles is conservation of life supporting systems and biodiversity by ensuring the sustainable use of renewable resources, so that the depletion of nonrenewable resources could be minimized. Conservation is the wise use of natural resources which allow future generations to enjoy natural resources which are necessary for our survival. Efficient use of natural resources and long term sustainability must be important aim of conservation of natural resources. Man because of his greed to procure more comforts is exploiting the nature. The sustainability goal is to raise the global standard of living without out increasing the use of resources beyond globally sustainable level; that is not exceeding one plane consumption. In this regard we should recollect Gandhiji's concept of 'non-possession'. Though he was not against state ownership of natural resources, he opposed individual/private ownership of such resources the main cause of which as mentioned earlier is increasing human needs and their complex way of life.

We cannot over look or ignore the fact that development / growth which will ultimately causes environmental degradation Since India is a developing country where the population growth rate is high , the problem of environmental degradation is mainly due to over consumption of goods and services. The situation in advanced courtiers is differ , as they could take various measures for maintaining environmental quality and have other alternatives and could maintain environmental sustainability. The following data based on Environmental Sustainability Index (ESI) gives a clear picture of India's position under ESI ranking at the national level . When we compare the position of India in the race of ESI ranking, India stood at low level of ESI. Environmental Sustainability Index reveals a comparative analysis of environmental achievement, challenges and priorities among Indian states, measures the potential of states to maintain their environment in the future decades given the various environmental resources that a state is endowed with. Tables 1 and 2 represents the ESI ranking of India and Andhra Pradesh . It clearly shows that ESI ranking of Andhra Pradesh goes up with the increased pressure on land and natural resources and deterioration of air and water quality.

Table - 1: Environmental Performance Index of the selected countries, 2010

Sl .No	*Countries*	*ESI Score*
1.	Switzerland	89.1
2.	France	78.2
3.	Australia	78.1
4.	UK	74.2
5.	Germany	73.2
6.	Japan	72.5
7.	USA	63.5
8.	Brazil	63.4
9.	India	48.3
10.	Pakistan	48.0
11.	Bangladesh	44.0

(*Source*: http:/www.greenindia standards.com)

The 2010 Environmental Performance Index (EPI) ranks 163 countries on 25 performance indicators covering both environmental public health and ecosystem vitality. The following table represents EPI of a few selected countries which reveals that India stood for relatively low ranking.

The above data witnessed the low levels of environmental sustainability in India in general and Andhra Pradesh at particular. Most of the European countries occupied the highest level of ESI rank ranging from 70 to 80 above, where as developing

Table - 2: Environmental Sustainability Index(ESI) of Andhra Pradesh in 2007, 2008 and 2009

Indicator	*ESI Score In 2007*	*ESI Score In 2008*	*ESI Score In 2009*
Population pressure	0.77	0.70	0.73
Land use and forestry	0.19	0.13	0.33
Natural resources endowments	0.16	0.29	NA
Natural resources depletion	0.19	0.58	NA*
Waste management	0.17	- 0. 68	NA*
Water quality	0.56	- 0.32	-0.79
Air quality	0.10	0.23	0.26
Health	0.02	0.16	-0. 09
GHG (Green House Gases)	1.42	1.08	NA*
People's initiatives	24	0.15	NA*
AP ESI Rank	0.70	23	40

(*Source:* http:/www.greenindia standards.com)

Note: Values are calibrated in a scale of 0 (worst) to 100 (best) -3 worst , + 3 best and 0 means average.

* NA – Data Not Available

countries like India (48.3) , Pakistan (48.0) and Bangladesh (44.0) ranking at lowest level.(T-1) . In case of Andhra Pradesh , during the three consequent years of 2007,2008 and 2009 ,AP stands in between 24 to 40 ESI ranking levels. The indicators of ESI scores like population pressure carries average (0.77, 0.70 and 0.73) , use of land and forestry scores worst ranking (-0.19, - 0.13 and -033), the score in case of natural resource depletion is also worst (-0.19, - 0.58) . There are a number of instances in our country where the so called economic development is brought by either depletion or destruction of natural resources and damaging the environment which threatens the life of humans and other living organisms.

In these circumstances, when we go through Gandhian ideologies or advocacies we can understand the reality of the environmental problems and able to find out the path for sustainable development .What all Gandhi had taught to people for their better living is rightly applicable to now a days situation. Gandhi was not only confined to a particular area of thought but his ideologies are extended to each and every field of knowledge. To say, Gandhi's ideology on environment or the need to protect the nature highlights his advocacies of trusteeship, the relationship of man with nature, economy of permanence which discourages reckless consumption of natural resources reveals his principles in consuming natural resources. For instance, Gandhiji had suggested us to live in harmony with nature. He believed that man has no power to create life; therefore he has no right to destroy life. Gandhiji views on the exploitation of nature clearly revealed in his famous saying that the 'earth has enough to satisfy everyone's needs but not every one's greed." He believed that man because of his greediness causes environmental degradation by over exploitation and reckless use of resources. As a result, apart from facing severe crises of depletion of natural resources at national level, we are combating with a crisis of global warming and ozone depletion at global front.

Gandhiji opinion on trusteeship system by which economic equality could be brought by a non-violent transformation through trusteeship process. i.e. a means to bring about a change and eliminate class conflict from social horizon, which would lead to equal partaking of benefits of natural resources for both rich and poor and thus no more depriving the poor of their bare minimum needs. This is very relevant to the state of affairs in our country today. Natural resources like land, forests ruled by private entities and corporate, whose use them for commercial benefits thereby depriving the public of natural resources. The large scale depletion of natural resources harm and inconvenience caused to the city life clearly endorses that natural resources should not be left to private ownership. In fact freely nature should be made accessible to all irrespective of the economic status. Depletion of natural resources increases the likelihood of 'resource wars'.

Gandhiji advocacy on 'Economy of Permanence' teaches us careful use of natural resources rather than reckless destruction for meeting present economic standards. In fact the activities by which the natural resources are being exploited to meet our present needs is thoughtless ; the result is that the future shows a dark picture for its availability . So usage of such resources in a sustainable manner is the need of the hour so that the future generations are not deprived of such precious ecological base.

To conclude, sustainable resource management focuses on human behaviour that encourages resources conservation and resource management activities that maintain both natural resources and the continued functioning of the ecosystem from which it is derived. While using the natural resources people must rethink the use of those resources, striving to reduce and ultimately minimize or eliminate their use. And also should know the importance of biodiversity and what we can do about endangered species of animals and plants in order to achieve the goal of sustainable development. There is no doubt that a large number of present day's environmental problems can be adequately addressed if Gandhi's teachings and doctrines are followed.

REFERENCES

1. Harold Hotelling, *The Economics of Exhaustible Resources,* 1931.
2. Gandhi, M.K (1950): *Hindu Dharma,* Navajivan publishing House Ahmedabad, p. 70.
3. Paper published on 'Caring for the Earth' IUCN, UNEP & WWF–1991.
4. *Gandhi Marg* (New Delhi) Oct.1988. *Collected Works of Mahatma Gandhi,* Vol. 88.
5. *Ibid; Collected Works of Mahatma Gandhi,* Ahmedabad; Navajivan Presss, 1958.
6. Mahajan, P.Mani and K.S.Bharati, *Foundations of Gandhian Thought,* Dattsons, Nagpur, 1987.
7. Daly, II.E (1990); "Towards some operational principles of sustainable Development" *Ecological Economics* 2:1-6
8. Little Green Book 2007, Publication of World Bank .
9. Global Foot Print Net work (2008); *"Living Planet" Reports,* retrieved on 1st October, 2008
10. Billon P (ed). (2005): *The Geopolitics of Resource Wars,* retrieved on 5th April 2009.
11. World Bank Report on "Strengthening Institutions for Sustainable Growth; Country Environmental Analysis for India, New Delhi, 10th April, 2007. http:/go.worldbank.org

http:www.greenindia standards.com

13

The Impact of Ghandhism on Indian English Literature with Special Reference to Select Novels

G. Chenna Reddy

Chaman Nahal is one of outstanding novelists of the seventies (1970's). He was born in 1927 in Sailkot in India. He worked as a professor of English at Delhi University. He was a Fullbright Fellow, Princeton University, New Jersey, from 1967 to 1970. He worked as lecturer at several universities in the USA, Malaysia, Japan, Singapore, Canada and North Korea; fellow, Churchil College. Cambridge from 1971 to 1991. He got Sahitya Academy Award in 1997 and Federation of Indian Publishers Award in 1979.

Chaman Nahal wrote 8 novels including, 'The Gandhi Quarter. He wrote "My Faaces in 1977, Into Another Dawn in 1977, The English Queens in 1979, Sunrise in Fiji in 1988, Azadi in 1975, The Crown and Loincloth in 1981. The Salt of Life in 1990, The Triumph of the Tricolor in 1993, The Gandhi: Quartet in 1993. The collection of Short Stories, The Weird Dance and others stories were published in 1965.

Chaman Nahal is a prominent contemporary fiction writer, who deals with Indian Freedom Struggle and the partition of the subcontinent into India and Pakistan in his novels. He designed The Gandhi Quartet to explore the incidents of freedom struggle and partition in a chronological order. In this sequence he divides the freedom struggle into three phases. The first three novels in The Quarter cover the actions and emotions of the people and the crucial incidents during the Non-Cooperation Movement, the Civil Disobedience and the Quit India Movement, while the fourth novel

I compiled on the pre-and post-partition riots at the Indo-Pakistan border during the separation of both the countries.

Some Indian novelists in English have dealt with a particular period or a particular incident of freedom movement in their novels. For example Raja Rao's Kanthapura is confined to a particular incident, i.e., the Non-Cooperation Movement and a particular South Indian small village Kanthapura though the novel is a saga of the freedom movement. It manifests the response of the common man to the Non-Cooperation Movement against the Crown. R.K. Narayana's Waiting for the Mahathma is another important novel, which deals with the freedom movement as background. The novel deals with some of the important incidents during the Quit-India Movement, where Gandhi is a character. Narayan also depicts the slow romantic love affair between Sriram and Bharati with the incidents of freedom movement as a backdrop.

Chaman Nahal's Quartet, which is a Gandhian Saga, deals with most of the major incidents and movements of the freedom struggle including the Non-Cooperation Movement during 1920 and 1922. Chaman Nahal himself observed in an article in the *Hindustan Times* that:

The Crown and the Loincloth deals with the first phase and I will have to write two more novels to project fully the Gandhian experiment if at all those novels are ever written.

The novel, The Crown and the Loincloth begins with the return journey of Gandhi from South Africa to India in the ship S.S. Arabia after the completion of his successful sojorn. He has successfully tested his newly found principle Satyagraha with which he fought against the British in South Africa.

Gandhi is not deeply involved in his family matters. Sometimes he feels guilty of his lack of love and affection towards his family. He spends most of his time in fighting against the problems of society-exploitation, slavery and untouchability. The guilt of negligence towards his family is reflected in the first part of the novel.

Gandhi spends most of his time in different agitations of the freedom movement. The British government put him in prison for many years. No, naturally, he does not have enough time to look after his children with fatherly affection.

Chaman Nahal weaves the historical characters with the fictional characters dramatically. He narrates the story of Thakur Santhi Nath a landlord and his large family in typical South Indian village, Ajith, in Punjab. The protagonist of the novel Sunil Kumar, a teacher, is the fourth son of Santhi Nath. Nahal has made Sunil Kuamr as the protagonist of the novel, though there are four sons and four daughters. Nahal has taken an educated native Sunil Kumar as protagonist to explore the Gandhian experiment in his novel, unlike Venkataramani who has taken Kandan as his protagonist in Kandan the Partiot.

He has more patriotic zeal than moral stigma. As a reaction to the call of Gandhi, he leaves his job and flings himself into the freedom struggle. The entire story of the novel moves around him. He is even ready to sacrifice his life to save the honour of the coutry. No doubt he is the protagonist of the novel in The Crown and the Loincloth.

> ....Sunil, the protagonist of the novel, comes under the enhancement of Mahatma Gandhi and becomes an active political worker (p. 40). Thakur Santhi Nath is an ambiguous character, who admires the British Rule and also believes in Gandhi. The grand old man looks after the entire family welfare and is troubled many a time by his family members. Santhi Nath has more responsibilities than any other character in the novel. As a landlord he has to show his loyalty to the Crown. At the same time, he should maintain the balance between his loyalty to the crown and the fight against the Crown by his son Sunil under the influence of the Loincloth.

Chaman Nahal introduces historical characters and events in the first chapter of the novel. Gandhi recollects the past incidents of his life as to how he spent two decades in South Africa and how he neglected to show love and affection towards his family members, while he was sailing from South Africa to India. The author confines to the narration of the historical characters and incidents at the opening chapter of the novel.

Nahal introduces the fictional characters in the second chapter. The large family of Thakur Santhi Nath, their typical Punjabi traditions, and culture, the honour and reputation of the family, their family relations, introduction of the protagonist Sunil Kumar and his wife Kusum, the revolutionist Rakesh and their involvement in the freedom struggle are vividly narrated in the second chapter. There is no logical coherence between the first and second chapter.

Again in the third chapter, Nahal narrates the historical event of Jallianwalla Bagh Massacre, but he weaves the historical characters and the fictional character. Sunil is injured severely, he is saved from death by Kenneth Ashby, who treats Indians as his brothren.

In the fourth chapter, the fictional story proceeds forward. Santhi Nath is bedridden because of the two major blows in his life: the elopements of Shyama, his daughter with Rakesh and the injuries of Suil Kumar. Sunil's conjugal life with Kusum and the lustful desire of Shyama are the major incidents at this juncture. The reactions of the villagers to those incidents, their sympathy and they enjoyment are the common in many Indian villages.

The important incidents that occur in the next chapter brings out the craftsmanship of Nahal, how he connects Sunil Kumar, the fictional character with the historical character-Gandhi. Once again the historical events are combined with the fictional actions. The meeting of Sunil Kumar with Gandhi at Amritsar gives a different turn to the story. Sunil leaves his job and becomes the Congress volunteer.

Gandhi's inability to love his family and his love and affection towards the motherland are brought out in the first part of the novel. Sunil's love and conjugal life with Kusum is narrated with an overdose of sex in this part. Shayma's affection towards Rakesh does not stop her to practice their family ethics and morals. Sunil is also equally immoral as he is attracted towards Rehana, a Congress volunteer, calling her as 'The Eternal Lover'. The patriotic zeal and the love and affection of their motherland attract Sunil, Kusum, Rehana, Rakesh and Muzaffar to participate in the freedom struggle.

The chapters from six to nine are under part-II-Perspectives, Nahal introduces an American woman Celia, a fictional character to show the American Sympathy and the attraction towards Gandhi and the freedom struggle . Chaman nahal says, that:

> .... Since no American was actively involved with the Gandhian Movement, I keep Celia Ashby strictly at the neutral level. But

through her presence, I try and project how Gandhi might have struck rest of the world. (p. 47)

Sunil is sent by the All India Congress to Simla Hills to solve the problems of the laborers. The tradition and culture of the tribals on the hilss is narrated in the part 'Perspectives'. The way of living of the people on the hills, their caste, creed, immortality and exploitation of the laborer, the immoral behavior of Sunil is narrated. Sunil Kumar has lead a virtuous life except for the flaw of weakness for women. He proved his valor when he was willing to sacrifice his life for the Prince of Wales in order to save the honour of the country. Gandhi opine, Sunil was a noble man. He died a noble death. (p.40)

The congress meets in Delhi to endorce the 'call off' of Non-Cooperation Movement by Gandhi. Though almost all the leaders oppose the ideas of Gandhi, he himself is confirmed that his decision is right. After the death of Sunil, Kusum takes a bold step to leave for Sabarmathi Ashram from Ajitha. But she does not know whether her decision is right or wrong. She has confirmed , her decision is right only after the tender reception of Gandhi and Katubai at the Ashram.

In the last chapter, where Nahal wants to conclude the novel, he imposes may incidents blending historical with fictional details. Gandhi's bitter experience in the 'call off' of the Non-Cooperation Movement at Delhi Congress Session on 25th February, 1920 is a historical incident. Though this session is not connected with the climax, Nahal wants to impose historical veracity at this juncture. The attack of Rakesh on the life of the Prince of Wales during his visit in Amritsar is the climax of the novel. Nahal gives an abrupt conclusion to the novel by the sacrifice of the life of the protagonist, Sunil to save the honour of his mother land.

Nahal develops the story imposing Gandhism, through the character of Sunil and extremism through the character of Rakesh simultaneously. Using historical incidents and actions, Nahal is inclined to accept the victory of Non-Cooperation Movement by Gandhi. The Salt of Life, published in 1990, is the second novel in the chronological order of the Quartet. It deals with the second phase of the freedom struggle during the Civil Disobedience Movement in the twenties and thirties, from Gandhiji release from jail, i.e., from 1929 to Indian's involvement in the Second World War. The plot of the novel deals with the core incidents of freedom struggle like Gandhi-Irwin Pact, Gandhi's participation in the Second Round Table Conference, his withdrawal from the Congress and retreat to Sevagram, the working of Provincial Autonomy in 1937-39, the widening Hindu-Mulsim rift and the involvement of India in the Second World War. While this is the background of the novel, the foreground is the domestic life of Kusum, her marriage with Raja Vishal Chand, their honeymoon tour of Kerala, their happy life at Lambini and the mysterious end of Raja Vishal Chand.

The actions and the incidents of the fictional characters are mingled with historical incidents to create a suitable emotional atmosphere of the fictional characters. The revolutionary activities of the freedom movement are used to maintain the balance of characters an incidents in the novel. As Srinivas Iyenger observes:

The fictional narrative centred in Kusum's second lease of life is but part of the story of *The Salt of Life*, for it is the back grounding and often overpowering Gandhi Saga that sets the pace and imparts the deeper meaning to the novel. (p. 174)

Kusum, the protagonist of the novel plays an important role in Gandhi's ashram at Sabarmati. She has been working as a teacher for six years here in the ashram. Gandhi discusses with Kusum about his future plans to design a strategy for the freedom movement. Vikram, the son of Kusum grows under the shadow of Gandi.

Gandhi wants to take the freedom movement close to the common men of the country. He decides to break the law of the government. So he takes a decision to launch the Salt Satyagraha in the classroom of Kusum, while she is teaching the students about mineral 'salt'.

The title 'Thc Salt of Life' is a phrase from the epigraph which is itself taken from Gandhi's words to Kusum. (p. 173)

He tells

I will walking to the seashore and I won't return to Sabarmati until India's freedom is won. (p. 47)

Gandhi asks Kusum to accompany him in the march. But

the words of Kusum have shocked at him she too leaves the ashram for other purpose.

Many revolutionary activists including Charulatha and Bhagat Singh are put in Lahore Central Jail. Nahal narrates the deplorable conditions of the jail vividly. Rakeh wants to help Charulatha and Bhagat Sing to escape from the jail as stays at a nearby village. Both Rakesh and Charulatha were sentenced to death for their attempt on the life of the Prince of Wales in 1922 in the previous novel The Crown and the Loincloth. But they together excepted from the jail a few months after their imprisonment and hid in Goa, which was a safe place for extremists.

Gandhi comes to know that Kusum wants to marry Raja Vishal Chand, the Prince of Lambini, and a small princely state in Jammu Kahsmir.

The Lambini had a close semantic resemblance with Lumbini, the place where Buddha was born. (p.89).

Vishal Chand stays for sometime at a bungalow near the ashram and attends the prayer meeting of the Ashram. A man of virtue and a disciple of the Gandhi, Vishal is attracted towards Kusum and he proposes for marriage. Gandhi, himself makes all arrangements for their marriage in the ashram. Though he gave his consent for the marriage of Bharathi and Sriram in Waiting for the Mahatma, it did not take place as he was assassinated on the previous days of the date of their proposed marriage. But in the case of Kusum and Vishal, it is materalised. Vishal wants to establish a high school in Lambini. Anjela Davis is a fictional character called from England to be the principal of the school.

Gandhi begins his Dandi march early in the morning on 12th March, 1930 from Sabarmati Ahsram with seventy-eight followers, the youngest being thirteen , to walk 240 miles to Dandi, the seacoast of the Arabian Sea, R.C. Majundar observes about the march of Gandhi.

> He decided to launch the Satyagraha Campaign by manufacturing salt at Dandi, a village on the sea coast in Gujarat about 200 miles from Sabarmati, and they by openly break the salt law.

Chaman Nahal artistically blends his fictional characters Kusum , Vishal Chand, Shyama and Rakesh with the historical persons like Gandhi, Kasturba and so on. K.R. Srinivas Iyengar observes:

> The ups and downs in the lives of fictional characters like Kusum and her friend Shyama, of their spouses and children and relations and friends, mingle with the events relating to historical figures like Gandhi, Kasturba, Congress leaders like Sardar Patel, Jawaharlal, Sarojini Naidu, Rajaji, Maulana Azad, and not – at other levels – with the destinies of Bhagat Singh and the revolutionary Subhas Bose who is enabled to effect a sensational escape to Europe soon after the outbreak of the 2nd World War. (p. 176)

Gandhi's prayers and his hymns from the Gita reveal the cultural background of the country. Hundreds of children and people are given education at Sabarmati ashram, like in Tagore's Santhi Nekethan.

Gandhi took a personal care about the welfare of orphans who lose their parents in freedom struggle. Kusum has been working as a teacher in the Ashram for a long time. Gandhi is attracted towards the discipline and commitment of Kusum and even he doesn't hesitate to take advice from this simple school teacher.

Chaman Nahal does not exploit history anywhere in the novel. He dramatically combines fiction with history. The novel begins after Gandhi's self imposed vow of political silence was over in 1929 and it ends with India's involvement in the World War II.

The historical revolutionary incidents play a significant role in the novel. The escape of Subhas Chandra Bose from India to foreign and his route of journey in the novel are historically true. But the involvement of Rakesh the fictional character and his revolutionary activities are fictional. The author weaves his fictional characters with the historical extremist incidents for his purpose.

Chaman Nahal created two groups of character like Kusum, Sunil, Raja Vishal Chand and their children are influenced by Gandhi and Rakesh the friend of Sunil is influenced by Sobash Chandra Bose. Here, Nahal artistically narrates incidents by the influence of both Gandhi and Bose simultaneously. His fictional creation moves around the principles of non-violence and extremism. Even the followers of Mahatma Gandhi are temporarily attracted towards Bose because of Gandhi's long absence in public who confined to jail. But ultimately they realized their folly and started to follow the Gandhi 'Marg'.

The protagonist of the Gandhi Quartet, Kusum and the protagonist of The Crown and the Loincloth Sunil are deeply influenced by Mahatma Gandhi. As Mahatma Gandhi could not care his family, the fictional heroes did the same. Though they faced dire consequences like deep wounds both physically and mentally they firmly took a decision to follow the footsteps of the symbolic loincloth, Mahatma Gandhi.

REFERENCES

1. Chaman Nahal, Telling of Time Past, *Hindustan Times*, March, 15, 1981, p. 12.
2. Chaman Nahal., *The Salt of Life*, Bombay; Allied Publishers Limited, 1990, p. 40, 47
3. Chaman Nahal, *The Crown and the Loincloth*, p. 422.
4. Dhawan, R.K., *Three Contemporary Novels, Khushwant Singh, Chaman Nahal and Salman Rushdie*, New Delhi, Classic Publishing Company, 1985, p. 162.
5. Mathur, O.P., *The Novels of Chaman Nahal, The Modern English Fiction*, 1987, p. 155
6. Majumdar, R.C., *History of the Freedom Movement in India*, Vol:III, Calcutta, Firma K.L. Mukhopadhyaya, 1963, pp. 335-36
7. Radha, K., *Azadi and The Crown and the Lioncloth three contemporary novelists*, Khushwant Singh, Chaman Nahal, Salman Rushdie, ed.
8. Srinivas Iyenger, K.R., *The Gandhian Saga Indian Literature*, September-October, 1991. p. 174.
9. *Ibid.*, p. 176.

14

Gandhi and His Weapon to Rebuild Society

K. Ravi Kumar, Ch.Ramakrishna & *K.Sridevi*

Gandhi, the Mahatma, is one of the rare humanists and social thinkers of the world. He was a social reformer and a worker par excellence who dedicated his life towards the cause of upliftment of the weaker sections, because he had the conviction that the real social reconstruction and a well-being of nay nation cannot be attained unless the needy , the deprived and the exploited people are uplifted and delivered social justice. As Gandhi put it, he wanted to construct an India in which he could 'wipe the tears from the face of the poorest in the land". Not only that, Gandhi always advocated the cause of the socially handicapped and deprived as well as the marginal man. Aurobindo rightly said, "There are philanthropists who would be troubled if the poor were not with us, for they would then have no filed for charity. But since Gandhi was a moralist and humanist, preacher of truth and non-violence, propagator of unity of mankind, benevolence and sacrifice for other, he advocated and practiced the means and principles of doing the good of others through voluntary actions by individual, associations and institutions as well. Gandhi's life and deeds speeches and writings, theories and models very much display his convictions in the philosophy of voluntary deeds which included doing welfare for others with the commitment to the principle of swadharms, without any expectation of gain in return out of that. Unnithan aptly remarks , 'what he desired was a conscious submission of the individual and a voluntary contribution of his possession to the society , which consisted of all, not a of a majority; and, in return the social system built upon the principles of non-violence and democracy, was to give a complete guarantee for the maximum development of his personality. The upliftment of the weaker sections constituted a vital task and an essential part of Gandhian programme of social reconstruction.

This paper is intended towards making a scrutiny of the Gandhian way of upliftment of downtrodden. The term downtrodden has been taken to mean here the group or class of people who are unable to solve their basic needs and are subjected to discrimination and exploitation. They live in abysmal condition and are deprived of rights, benefits and privileges. The destitutes, the Girijans, or untouchables are Gandhi's Daridranarayans, the beggars and any other socially handicapped groups of people constitute the class of downtrodden.

The care, protection and betterment of the weaker sections have ever been the responsibility of the state and society at large. But individuals and organizations too, always have made efforts to protect, uplift and solve the problems of the weaker sections. At this point, it would be proper to clarify the annotation of the term voluntary organization which is devoted to the cause of voluntary or self motivated action for the purpose of solving problems of rescuing and giving relief to any individual group and society. Voluntary action and organization are based on the philosophy of philanthropy , charity and moral obligations to serve and sacrifice for others.

It does not need elaboration that voluntary organizations are involved in extending aid and charity to the needy. Besides , they provide different types of protections to the people confronted with problems. Voluntary organizations are involved in generating social harmony and fellow-feeling among the individuals of society. Charity in the sense of mutual aid, solidarity, sociability and unselfish feeling of benevolence towards others can be said to exist among the crudest and moral primitive human societies and even may groups of bird, mammals and insects. Darwin in his *Descent of Man*, has remarked on man's physical weakness, being more than counterbalanced partly by his intellectual faculties and partly by his social qualities leading him to give and receive aid from his fellow-men. The tradition of giving charity to the needy and protecting the helpless is thus as old as human society.

References of such acts by voluntary organizations can be traced back to the ancient days in almost all the societies of the world. The Greek, Roman, Christians, Chinese and Indians right from the ancient to the present time have been found involved in doing some forms of philanthropy for the needy and the downtrodden. In all the religions, clear-cut prescriptions have been laid down to extend help and protection to the deserving needy. Such acts of any people or organization have been put under the category of social service and social work. In fact, the service of a needy is a part of long tradition in India. Like in other societies the case of the needy was built into the structure of social institutions. Religion as said above prescribed and emphasized the values of charity, philanthropy and mutual aid. The giving of alms, the feeding and care of destitutes were considered the acts of religious merit. The temples gave shelter to the homeless. Social institutions also provided mechanisms to meet the needs of the old, the sick, and other helpless sections of the community. The joint family, caste and community councils as well as the state were often philanthropic deed has been continuing until now. But some of them have become non-fucntional in the realm of voluntary actions for the needy.

However, the advent of British rule caused ushering a new era of philanthropy, social service and social reform in India. The arrival of Christian missionaries and western ideas aroused the feeling and motivated some Indians to initiate the process of social reform and extricate the weaker sections from their semi-human condition. As a consequence, a number of voluntary organizations came into being to pursue the said purpose. Raj Rammohun Roy, perhaps , is the first person in modern India, who took up the cause of the downtrodden. As a social reformer, he pleased for the abolition of caste distinctions and the practice of sati. Founder of the Brahmo Samaj, he also established many educational institutions. Afterward, Dwaraka Nath Tagore, Devendranath Tagore, Keshab Chandra Sen, Ranade, Rama Bai, Phule and host of others took up the cause of social reform not only for the reconstruction of modern India but also for the sake of the upliftment of the weaker sections. Obviously their efforts led to emergence of a number of voluntary organizations in India. The prominent among them were Brahmo Samaj, Prarthana

Samaj, Anjuman-e-Himayat-e Islam, Arya Samaj, Ramakrishna Mission, Theosophical Society. Etc. The tradition of social reform and establishment of voluntary organizations continued in the 20th century because of Gokhale, Tilak and other giant social reformers including Mahatma Gandhi.

Appearance of Gandhi on Indian scene in early part of this century virtually brought new hopes and aspirations as well as bright future for the weaker sections., namely, harijans, girjans, sudras , lepers, women and all those who could be kept under the rubric of weaker sections. infact, Gandhi gave prime consideration to dispel any form of inequality and exploitation . Swaraj for him not needy – the daridranarayan who suffer from hunger , disease and exploitation. Gandhi's constructive programme, sarvodaya and trusteeship contain the principles and means to secure social justice to the down trodden. Likely his theory of untouchability and others provide clues and framework for philanthropic deeds for the socially handicapped. Gore and Soares write, his constructive programme was both a movement for economic betterment and promoting the tenor of social life. To stress the common duties of men and women, and not equal rights of women alone, was characteristic of his approach to social reforms. So also he did not teach in terms of the harijans but of the duties of the higher castes towards them. He believed that an emphasis on right divides, whereas an emphasis on duties serves to unite.

There is no denying the fact that a number of voluntary organizations were engaged in making efforts to uplift the downtrodden. But Gandhi took up the cause of untouchables, sudras , women, tribals lepers and the poor in general irrespective of their caste and occupation. Gandhi did many voluntary works for the aforesaid downtrodden. However, his special contribution in the organizational field was to set up the appropriate national organizations with dedicated personnel to solve specific problems, for example, the Harijan Sevak Sangh, the All India Village Industries Association, the Nai Talim Sangh (basic educational movement,) etc.,

In addition to institution founded and supported by Gandhi he inspired a large number of voluntary activities directed towards social reform by individuals and organizations. Obviously , during the lifetime of Gandhi and in post-independence era, numerous voluntary organizations have come up by now. The estimated number of which is more than 3 lakhs in our country and included 10,000 such organizations in Andhra Pradesh. These voluntary organizations are of two categories, namely government aided and non government aided organizations. Besides , both these two types of organizations get or do not get aid from foreign agencies.

The works and efforts of the voluntary organizations have made significant contributions to the cause of reduction of poverty, untouchability, child labour, bonded labour, expansion of education. Opportunity of work for the needy, protection of the tribals, rehabilitation of exploited women, welfare of the beggars, medical treatment of lepers and others, etc... Gandhiji's Swaraj bore three hallmarks – unity among Indians of all religions, but particularly between Hindus and Muslims, the eradication of untouchability, and the practice of swadeshi. Gandhi in his political career showed a deep understanding of Indian social problems concerning all aspects of life, such as social , political, economic and cultural and spiritual. He combined constructive work and social reforms with his political programmes. His main emphasis was on the development of the poor mass through governmental as well as voluntary effort. His all concept of swadeshi, sarvodaya and trusteeship was based on volunteerism. In fact, political activities and social work were two sides of the same coin. He took up the cause of the Harijans and women. He campaigned for the constructive work for the downtrodden people throughout his life. He laid foundation for the Harijan Sewak Sangh, Gramodyog Sangh and Hindustan Talim Sangh and Sewagram, as a part of his constructive programme. Thus he combined in his work social reform, economic betterment and political upliftment.

During the freedom struggle, a large band of dedicated workers inspired and influenced by Gandhi took to constructive work and made it their life's mission and spread it throughout the country. On the whole, the Gandhian society was to be based on mutual cooperation and self-help. By reducing the state authority through expansion of voluntary social activity, he aimed at creating a democracy based on the welfare of not the majority but of all in the society. In creation of such a society he emphasized service and sacrifice as the motivating forces. Gandhi envisaged building up of a society, beginning with making villages self-sufficient in every manner, which partake the character of republics, and India as a whole was to be a republic of republics. He holds:

> 'I shall work for an India in which the poorest shall feel that it is their country, in whose making they have an effective office; an India in which there shall be no high class and low class people; an Indian in which all communities shall live in peace and harmony... this is the India of my dream.'

The ultimate idea of Gandhian philosophy has been the creation of a cooperative commonwealth leading to sarvodaya. He never spelt out his sarvodaya. As Vinobaji pointed out, while sarvodaya was more comprehensive concept, its core consisted of Antyodaya – the rise of the poorest, lowliest. Gandhi picked up ideas in his early years from Ruskin's, *Unto the Last*. There will be deliberate suppression of insatiable wants of human beings. At the same time, however, there will be human contentment because the minimum needs would be satisfied for all human beings and not for a few.

REFERENCES

1. B.S. Gupta , *Education and Integration in the Tribune,* Chandigarh.
2. M.K.Gandhi, *To Students*, Navajivan Publications House, House, Ahmedabad, 1953.
3. Ratan Das, *The Global Vision of Mahatma Gandhi*, Sarup & Sons, New Delhi, 2005.
4. Ashu Pasricha, *Gandhi in Twenty-First Cenruty*, Deep & Deep Publications Pvt. Ltd. New Delhi, 2011
5. Savepalli Radhakrishnan, *Mahatma Gandhi, Essays & Reflections*, Jaico Publishing House, Mumbai, 1957.
6. Louis Fischer, *Mahatma Gandhi: His Life & Times,* Bharatiya Vidhya Bhavan, 2006
7. Shesharao Chavan, *Mahatma Gandhi, The Sole Hope and Alternative*, Bharatiya Vidhya Bhavan, 1996.
8. Romain Rolland, *Mahatma Gandhi*, Rupa & Co, New Delhi2007
9. Robert Payne, *The Life and Death of Mahatma Gandhi*, Robert, Rupa & Co, New Delhi, 2003

Index

Acharya Ramamurty Committee
on Education, 91

AICTE, 89

All India Village Industries
Association, 132

Antyodaya, 134

Aparigraha, M., 15

Asteya, 17

Aurobindo, 129

Azad Hind League, 21

Balais of Maharashtra, 29

Basic education,
salient features, 88

Bhagwad Gita, 99

Bharat Yatra Kendras, 5

Bhave, Vinoba, 51

Bhoodan,
and Gramdan, 53

Bose, Gandhi and Ambedkar,
their ideology, 20-25

Brahmo Samaj, 131

Buddha, 19

CABE, 86

Caring of Earth, 115

Chakwara incident, 30

Chaturvarnya system, 32-33

Chennaiah, B., 93

China, 5

Choodamani, S.V.G., 36

Clinton, Bill, 109

Communal harmony, 108

Constructive programmes, 51

Dalits, 27, 56
strengthening and developing,
56

Development,
basic values of, 49

Dharmana, Rama Rao, 84

Dharmpal, 75

Education, 84
basic, 87
Gandhian philosophy of, 85

ESI, 115

Galbraith, J.K., 15

Gandhi Seva Sangh, 74

Gandhi, Mahatma, 45
as communicator, 50
and environment, 51
and Satyagraha, 62
and social action, 68-83
and his weapon to rebuild
society, 129-134
background, 57
basic philosophy of, 61
concept of renunciation, 46
concept of work and culture,
77

contribution of to Indian society, 57-67
on social values, 48
on non-violence, 48
practical idealist, 72
philosophy of education, 85
Talisman, 73
to students, 76

Gandhian ideals,
relevance of, 39

Gandhian ideology,
relevance to contemporary society,45

Gandhian thought,
Lohia's extension of , 3-10

GATS, 89

Gita, 47

Global crisis,
Gandhi and Lohia on, 11-19

Global menace,
fighting against, 107

Global village, 104

Globalisation, 88
advantages of, 89
and education objective, 89
and Gandhian perspective, 103
Gandhian perspective, 102-112
impact of on education, 90
role of value education in context of, 84-92

Gore, 132

Gram Swaraj, 106-107

Gramodyog Sangh, 133

Gulipilli, Rajeswari, 84

Hariprasad, A., 20

Hindus,
Ambedkar's views on future religion of, 26-35

Hindustan Talim Sangh, 133

Hindustan Times, 121

HIV/AIDS, 108

Human rights and environment, protecting, 55

Hussain, Zakir, 86

Hygiene and sanitation, 82

Indian English literature,
impact of Gandhism on, 120-128

Indian National Congress, 21

Indian Opinion, 70

Iswarbhai Patel Committee, 87

Iyengar, K.R. Srinivas, 127

Iyer, Raghavan, 111

Iyer, Saraswati Raju, 57

JCV Science Foundation, 11

Johannesbug, 71

JP, 18

Kavitha incident, 30

Krishnamurthy, V., 68

Kumar, K. Ravi, 129

Kumar, P. Kishore, 93

Lohia, Ram Manohar, 3-10

Luxemburg, Rosa, 5

Macaulay, 69

Manu, 27

Marx, Karl, 23

Mehta, Asoka, 4

Mohan, Surendra, 3

Nahal, Chaman, 121

Nai Talim,68

Narayan, Jai Prakash, 3

National Conference of Socialist Party, 4

National education,
  and craft-oriented education, 81

Natural resources, sustainable management of,
  relevance of Gandhian principles for, 113-119

NBA, 49

Netaji,
  and Gandhi, 22

Non-violence,
  Gandhi's views on, 36-41

Oxford University, 11

Poor and oppressed,
  to work with, 54

Primary education,
  universalisation of, 107

PSW, 47

PSW, 55

Pulla Rao, S., 113

Quit India movement, 121

Radhakrishnan, Sr. 33

Raju, M. Lakshmipathi, 45

Ramakrishna, CA., 129

Rao, K. Ananda, 102

Rao, K. Visweswara, 102

Rao, RVLN Ratnakara, 68

Rath, Bhagwat Prasad, 11

Reddy, G. Chenna, 120

Reddy, K. Raghu Ram, 20

Renede, Prof. S.N., 55

Roy, M.N., 18

Ruskin, 70-71

Saiyidain, K.S., 79

Sarvodaya,
  and social work, 53

Satyagraha, 63, 72
  and passive resistance, 64
  Gandhi's view on, 64
  principles of, 64
  practicability of, 66
  techniques of, 65

Schopenhauer, 74

Self-discipline, 75

Self-sufficiency, 106

Sex education, 108

Social service,
  Gandhi's interest in, 59

Social work
  acting as communicators, 55
  and Sarvodaya, 61
  revamping, 54

South Africa, 57

Sridevi, K., 129

Sudhakar, Ch. Y., 26

Sustainable development, 106

Thakkar, A.V., 51
The Salt of Life, 125
Tolstoy Farm, 71
Trade Union Movement, 58
Tutu, Desmond, 102

UNESCO Commission, 87, 88
Unnithan, 129
Unto The Last, 59, 71, 134
Untouchability, 26
USA, 5
Usha, P., 113

Value-oriented reforms, 92
Vinoba, 134
Voluntary action, 130

WTO, 5, 6, 7

Young India, 77
Youth and global peace,
  Gandhian perspective, 93-101
Youth,
  as agent for community
    renovation, 94